BEER CRAFTS

MAKING THE MOST OF YOUR CANS, BOTTLE CAPS, AND LABELS

Shawn Gascoyne-Bowman

Andrews McMeel
Publishing, LLC
Kansas City • Sydney • London

BEER CRAFTS

Andrews McMeel Publishing, LLC
an Andrews McMeel Universal company
1130 Walnut Street, Kansas City, Missouri 64106
www.andrewsmcmeel.com

13 14 15 16 17 TEN 10 9 8 7 6 5 4 3 2 1

ISBN: 978-1-4494-2783-2

Library of Congress Control Number: 2012951369

CONTENTS

THANKS

This book couldn't have been made without the help of a number of talented, smart, and funny people. My heartfelt thanks go to all the fabulous folks at Andrews McMeel who turned this project into a real book, with a special shout-out to Lane Butler and Holly Ogden. Additional thanks go to: Sorche, Bo, Xander, and Lucy, the folks who've always got my back; Matt Newell, for pattern templates; Bekki Scotto, for original hat pattern designs; Emily Engdahl, for her kind thoughts and words; Elizabeth Start, for the loan of one spectacular dress; Amy Honeyman and Keri Pieh, for help with project designs; Orange Show Center for Visionary Art, for the use of photographs and biographical information about John Milkovisch; project and pattern testers Shelly Pagliai, Anne Wilseck, Donna Bartelt, and Felix Hewison-Carter. Even more thanks to Alex Ganum for trusting me with the keys to the brew house and lots of inspiration. My neighbors Jason and Dana were kind enough to take beer off my hands when I needed cans emptied. Way to take a hit for the team, guys! And, of course, thanks to Katie Merritt and all the folks at SCRAP.

Laura Sams's and Rob Sams's contributions to *Beer Crafts* extend way beyond photography; they've been supportive, creative collaborators, darling models, and great friends.

I'm hugely grateful to my good-looking friends who let me shanghai their afternoons for impromptu modeling sessions: Casey White, Bo Bowman, Bobby Roberts, Matt Newell, Cris Martin, Giuseppe Lipari and his girl Jane, Sue McDonald, Leslie Mestman, Ryan Manner, Jennifer Dawkins, and Brandy Ethridge are good sports, and I owe you all a beer!

Thanks to Upright Brewing, Taylor's Market, Beer Bunker, Caldera Public House, and Montevilla Station for the use of their space for photographs.

A highlight in making this book was enjoying the fine beers used in the crafts. An enormous thanks to the following breweries and organizations who gave permission to use images: Pabst Blue Ribbon, New Belgium Brewing, Fearless Brewing Company, 21st Amendment, Fort George

Brewery, Upright Brewing, Jacob Leinenkugel Brewing Company, Rabbit's Foot Brewing, Unita Brewing, Maui Brewing Co., The Pike Brewing Company, Hale's Ales, Schirf Brewing Company, Lagunitas Brewing Company, Ninkasi Brewing Company, Uncommon Brewers, Kona Brewing Company, Big Sky Brewing, Full Sail Brewing, Avery Brewing, Shmaltz Brewing Company, Green Flash Brewing Company, North Coast Brewing, Brouwerij Van Steenberge, Boulder Beer, Laurelwood Brewing, Women Enjoying Beer, Magic Hat, Laurelwood Brewing Company, and Avery Brewing Company.

FOREWORD

When the crafty and craft beer communities come together, we all win. Creativity and crafting with found objects, including reusing bottle caps, cans, bottles, and carriers, is a direct expression of the craft beer philosophy that creates community around sustainability.

This sustainability, coupled with creativity, repurposing, and innovation, are all ways in which we can support our local communities, and in turn, the earth. When we support craft brewers, we keep dollars in our neighborhoods, strengthening our local economy. When we craft using repurposed materials, we keep waste out of the refuse stream and find unusual sources for supplies. In both beer and art, we are given glorious opportunities to build relationships with others, and expand our creative horizons. What better way to complement each other than by crafting with beer?

This is the heyday of the do-it-yourself mentality. From urban farming to home brewing, from the resurgence of modern domesticity like beautifully home sewn clothing to handmade objects for the home, the can-do attitude of creative folks is the very same industriousness that spurred on the craft beer movement from home brewers in the early 1980s.

At the very core, the hearts of craft beer and crafting beat with the same fundamental tempo. Within these two, community is queen. So grab a beer, gather up some friends, and get to it. There's nothing better than enjoying a tasty beverage while creating, laughing, and having a good time with your friends. This book will show you the way!

Emily Engdahl

Crafter, home brewer, beer writer

Owner-creator, Oregon Beer Country

INTRODUCTION

Crafting may be my first love, but beer and I have a long and passionate history. Thank goodness, appreciating them both doesn't have to be a rivalry for affections and I can enjoy them simultaneously, sometimes even in public.

I'm amazingly fortunate to be living in Portland, Oregon, which has the largest number of breweries per capita in the United States, and the beers here are pretty darn good—right up there with the awesome brews coming from my hometown of Fort Collins, Colorado. But I'm guessing you've got some kick-ass beers in your town, too. It's a plague of awesomeness.

We've seen a revolution in crafting and knitting. Folks are learning to make things for themselves again, and luckily for us they've rediscovered beer. Home brewers who have been experimenting with hundred-year-old German recipes are opening brewpubs, and outstanding craft breweries are popping up all over the country—really, all over the world.

Innovative graphic design has accompanied the boom in the beer industry, with stunning packaging acting as a visual signature from the breweries. My appreciation for these cool cans and subsequent collection of them had turned into a bit of a problem. These things take up space, and a couple of years ago it seemed time to move on from my decorating style of "dorm room chic" to something more befitting a foxy middle-aged mom.

The answer to the question, "What do you do with the ninety-nine beers on the wall?" came from an unlikely source, my eight-year-old daughter. She had become obsessed with making jewelry out of my discarded bottle caps, and one morning, I found a note on my desk that said, "My crafting involves you to open a beer." Suddenly I had an epiphany:

My Crafting
Involves
you to
Open a
beer

"*ALL* crafting should involve my opening a beer." The basic source materials for dozens of craft projects are right in my house, no farther than the fridge or recycle bin.

Take cans, for example: The perfect delivery system for getting the fresh, tasty goodness from the brewery to my mouth is still a perfect, usable *thing* once you've drained the contents, and chances are it's pretty, and like so many of us, it has potential!

With this in mind, I raised my daughter's allowance and set down to writing this book. But first, I opened a beer. As a tribute to the beer books I love to read, I've divided projects and chapters up by the style of beer that inspired them, working as you might do at a tasting, moving from lightest beer to darkest.

So, grab a bowl of pretzels, invite your friends over, and remember: You'll be working with sharp pointy things here, and hot glue, so please drink and craft responsibly.

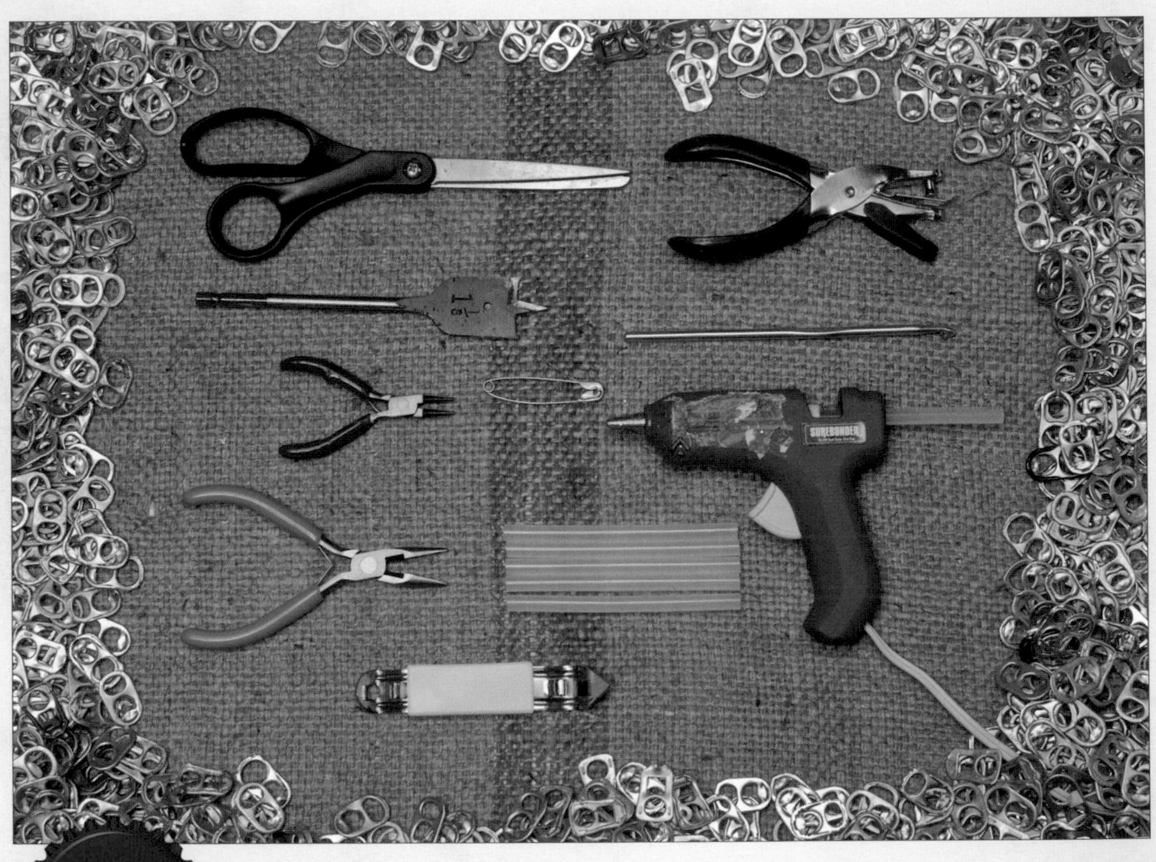

WORKING WITH CANS AND CAPS

Aluminum Cans

After spending a couple of years playing around with cans, I'm completely convinced they are one of the most versatile and underused building materials we have in abundant supply. Easily cut and manipulated, the cans are an uncomplicated medium. You can poke little holes in them for jewelry jump rings or use a larger paper punch to make holes for crocheted hats and bags. The material is light and flashy, and you've got an endless palette of colors to choose from, depending on your taste in beers. Some really talented artists are creating design work for cans right now. San Francisco's 21st Amendment, Maui Brewing in Hawaii, and Big Sky Brewing in Montana come immediately to mind.

GETTING STARTED

Cutting up a beer can is a lot easier than you might think. I've seen some tutorials in which folks put on heavy work gloves and use tin snips, which seems so over the top. My basic tools are a can opener and a pair of old scissors with a pointed tip. You might also include a spade bit from a drill (but not the drill itself) for puncturing and widening holes, a dedicated set of manicure scissors for more detailed work, and some thumbtacks. Because I cut lots of cans, I've set aside one pair of scissors for this purpose. Once you start hacking a lot of aluminum, they won't be much good at cutting paper or fabric afterward. The spade bit is something you'll need to hunt down at the hardware store. It's a drill attachment with a triangular blade that increases in size ending, in a flat surface. I use this *by hand* to punch holes in cans because it's got more surface area than a nail and doesn't crush the can when I push it in. The cans are so easy to cut and manipulate that you won't need the actual drill to make or expand holes.

Using gloves should be at your discretion. It's possible to cut yourself with an aluminum edge, but raw edges are infinitely less menacing than they at first appear. Cans do get little metal slivers, which I trim away immediately before working with them in depth, and I clean up the scraps from my craft room floor because I'd hate to step on one.

OPENING ON OUTSIDE EDGE

OPENING ON INSIDE EDGE

CUTTING CANS

To start my basic can deconstruction, I use a can opener on the *outside* edge of the can. This takes the whole top off, leaving me with a raw edge of aluminum exposed. If I'm planning to use the can to hold tools or art supplies, or as a pincushion, I open it on the *inside* edge, keeping the metal lip on top intact.

Once the top is off the can, I cut a vertical line down the length of the can, usually through the UPC code area. If I need a flat piece of aluminum to make a hat panel or piece of jewelry, I make an additional cut around the base of the can to remove the bottom section.

Bottle Caps

Along with cut aluminum from cans, bottle caps are the real workhorses of this book, either as stand-alone jewelry pieces such as earrings, pendants, or cufflinks, or as complements to larger projects, such as buttons on a bottle cozy or a dog jacket. I keep a funky old mason jar on my desk, overflowing with favorite caps. Even sitting like that it looks great, like a gumball machine for grown-ups, filled with memories of great beers tasted with friends.

GETTING STARTED

Find an awesome beer with an eye-catching cap. Decisions, decisions. You may want to stock up on extra beer in case you have a "craft fail." (The likelihood of a "craft fail," especially when working with caps, is pretty slim, so at this point I'm helping you justify the well-stocked fridge to the folks you might be cohabitating with.)

FILLING CAPS

I'm by no means a crafts purist, but I do like my projects to have a clean and finished look. I take special care not to bend the caps when I open a beer. You may want to buy a flat-topped bottle opener from the grocery store for just this purpose. When you pull off the cap, work your way slowly around the edges, lifting just a little bit each time you pry the sides away from the bottle. The force of carbon dioxide escaping from the beer is going to help the cap come off cleanly if you've loosened it all the way around.

After you've pried off the cap, savor your first sip—you've earned it—and remember:

BEER ISN'T JUST A GREAT CRAFT PROJECT WAITING TO HAPPEN. IT'S A FULL-BODIED, TASTY DRINK, TOO!

Dry off your cap and plug in your glue gun. Finding an ideal work space is critical. Pick a spot with good lighting, close to an outlet, with enough room to craft comfortably and an area for the hot caps to cool. I like to prep a whole bunch of caps ahead of time with glue, as the technique is the same for a lot of projects where you want to see the design side of the cap. You'll go through a lot of glue sticks filling caps, so make sure you've got lots of supplies on hand.

Fill your caps three-quarters of the way full with glue. You want to make sure to leave some room at the top of your cap to lay in magnets or jewelry hardware along with another thin layer of glue, and that there is space for these items lay flush with the top rim of the cap.

Your glue caps should be cool in five to ten minutes. Resist the urge to touch or move them until then. The metal caps conduct heat, and these puppies get very hot! You could use other types of glue but I've got no patience waiting overnight or longer for liquid glues to dry. With this technique, a number of crafts in the book can be completed in about fifteen minutes, which is perfect for making that last-minute birthday gift.

Lagers

A TRUSTED FRIEND AND SIDEKICK, LAGERS ARE THE QUINTESSENTIAL COOLER COMPANION, FRIDGE FRIEND, AND BARBECUE STAPLE. THE CRAFTS IN THIS CHAPTER SALUTE THE MOST BREWED AND CONSUMED STYLE OF BEER IN THE WORLD.

SHIFT
SHIFT
Pabst Blue Ribbon

Beer Can Awards

From "Master Home Brewer," to "Top Dad," or "Best Burp on the Block," someone in your life is due a very special blue-ribbon award. Beer can rosettes are a stunning way to let your pals know they are number one in your book. Pin a bunch on his jacket for that crazed dictator look, or pass out a handful to your whole platoon. They are quick and easy to put together, and once you've made one, you'll want to make dozens. Look for cans with lots of stripes, stars, and solid-color blocks. You'll probably want to sample a number of cans for this–lucky you! Viva la Beer Revolución!

Supplies

SCISSORS

SEVERAL BEER CANS

HOT GLUE GUN

PIN BACK (from a jewelry supply shop or craft store)

PUSHPIN (optional)

JUMP RINGS, for hanging the medals (optional)

1 Use the can opener and scissors to remove the top and bottom from each can. Trim the cool designs from your cans. Pick a large piece to be the focal part of your ribbon, and hot glue other, smaller pieces as embellishments either in front of or behind it.

2 Hot glue the pin back to the award.

3 Alternatively, if you'd like your award to be a dangling medallion or hang from a ribbon, you can poke holes in the aluminum with a push pin and connect the pieces with a jump ring.

Beer Can Trophies

They aren't very structurally sound, but old trophies hacked and rebuilt using beer cans sure look cool. Due to their delicate nature, you'll want to carry them from underneath and keep them far away from rowdy friends.

How to

1 Deconstruct your old trophy. A large screw and hex nut are probably holding the pieces together at the base.

2 Hot glue the empty cans to the trophy base and add some bling to the top of the highest can.

SUPPLIES

TROPHY from thrift store, **OR BLOCK OF WOOD**

1 TO 3 BEER CANS

HOT GLUE GUN

TROPHY BLING, such as brass cups or metal wreaths from the tops of deconstructed trophies

INDIA PALE ALE
Pabst
SHIFT
SHIFT

Cut-Can Wind Spinners

Nothing beats hanging out on the porch with friends and enjoying a cool brew and fresh breeze on a sunny day. These garden art wind spinners are the perfect house accessory for those lazy summer afternoons. You'll need a six-pack to make a string of three spinners, so invite your posse over. It's a quick and easy project, and fun to make with a bunch of folks while chillin' on the veranda.

1 Using the wire cutters, cut five 6-inch sections of wire and set aside. If you are using tall boy cans, you'll want 8-inch wire sections instead.

2 Using the pliers, bend a 1/4-inch-diameter round loop into one end of each wire segment.

3 Using the can opener on the outside of each can, remove the top. Mark eleven cut lines every 3/4 inch around the top of a can. Mark corresponding lines every 3/4 inch around the bottom of the can, to act as guides.

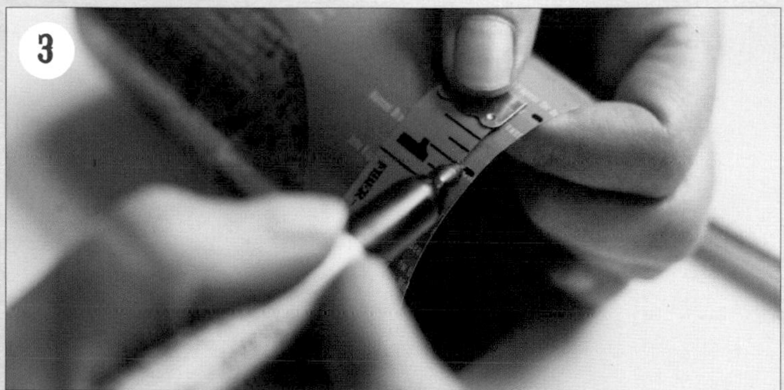

SUPPLIES

WIRE CUTTERS

RULER

30 INCHES OF 16-GAUGE MULTIPURPOSE UTILITY WIRE (40 inches if using tall boy cans), plus sufficient wire to hang the finished spinner

PLIERS

CAN OPENER

6 BEER CANS

FELT-TIP MARKER

SCISSORS

HAMMER AND NAIL

SPADE BIT FROM DRILL

3 LARGE, GLOBE-SHAPED BEADS with a hole large enough to slide over the wire

9

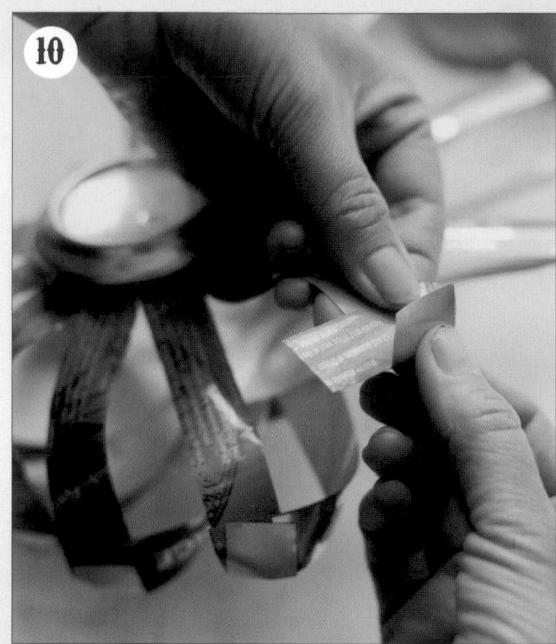
10

11

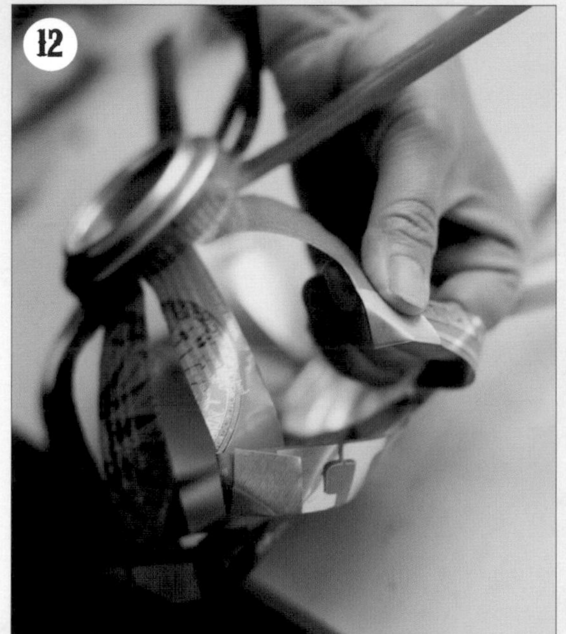
12

4 Use the scissors to cut eleven vertical slits down the length of the can from top to bottom.

5 Fold out the flaps flat like the petals of a flower.

6 Lay the can on a hard surface, such as scrap wood, with the label of the can facing you. Use the hammer and nail to pierce the center of the can bottom.

7 Repeat steps 3 through 6 with each remaining can.

8 By hand, use the spade bit drill attachment to expand the holes slightly in three of the cans so the holes are ⅛ inch in diameter (about the same size as a hole made by a standard paper punch).

9 From here, you'll be attaching two cans together. Take a can with a larger hole and rest it on the table, label side down. Take another can with a smaller hole and rest it on top with the label side up. Take a flap from the top can and lay it perpendicularly underneath a corresponding flap from the bottom can ¼ inch from the tip, as shown. The labels from each flap should be facing out.

10 Making a crease away from your body, fold the top can's flap over the bottom flap.

11 Fold the bottom can's flap toward you over the top flap.

12 Bend the point where the two cans meet slightly away from you. This will help keep the two cans attached and make them more aerodynamic. Repeat for the ten remaining flaps.

13 Thread one bead onto one piece of wire, sliding it down to rest on the loop. Repeat with two more wires.

14 Slide a spinner onto each wire with the larger hole can first, so it rests on top of the bead.

15 Attach the three spinners together by threading the top of one spinner loop into the bottom of another.

16 Use the additional wire to make a hook for the wind spinner and hang outside.

TRADEMARK
NEW YORK

Pull-Tab Bracelet and Belt

A million years ago, beer cans had completely different systems for opening. In my dad and granddad's day, you needed a special tool—the lethal-looking church key—to open them. When I was little there was a pull tab with a ring in the top, which would yank free, taking a triangle of the aluminum top with it. My buddies and I would fold these pop-tops together into chains for jewelry and belts. One year, we made a chain long enough to string as a garland for the Christmas tree, and a merry holiday that was!

You can still string today's tabs together. It's still a pretty hip fashion statement with the younger set, though these days you'll need to supply some ribbon for it. Transparent elastic thread is also great to use on a bracelet, as it makes it hard to tell just how exactly the pieces are bound together. I have also used a thin strip of old bike tire wound through pull tabs to make a long, punk-inspired belt. Cut strips of an old T-shirt work great, too.

This is one of my favorite crafts in the book, as you need to collect a fair number of cans. The jewelry isn't just for the ladies in the house, either. Pull-tab bracelets look fierce on guys, too.

1 Open a beer, but pay attention. The first couple of steps are going to require some concentration. When in doubt, refer to the photos.

2 Fold your ribbon in half lengthwise. From the front, slide the ribbon ends all the way through the top and bottom holes of a tab, as shown.

Supplies

✻ For a Bracelet ✻

30 INCHES OF 1/4-INCH-WIDE OR NARROWER RIBBON

25 TO 30 PULL TABS
for a lady's bracelet, or 30 to 35 to fit a guy's wrist

✻ For a Belt ✻

100 INCHES OF 1/4-INCH-WIDE RIBBON OR STRIPS OF THIN T-SHIRT FABRIC

100 PULL TABS
(to fit a 35-inch waist)
For a larger belt, increase your tab count by 3 additional tabs per inch.

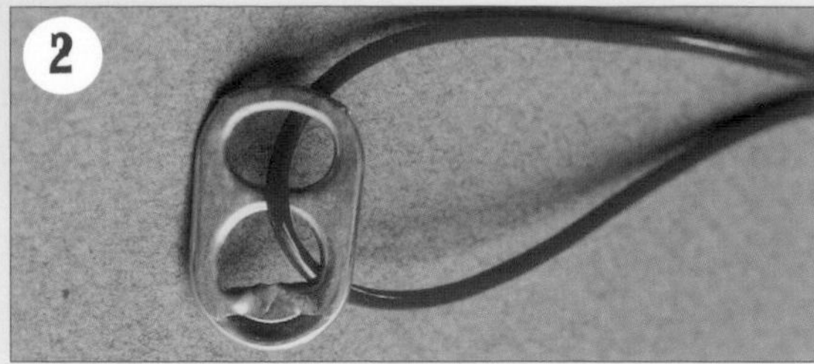

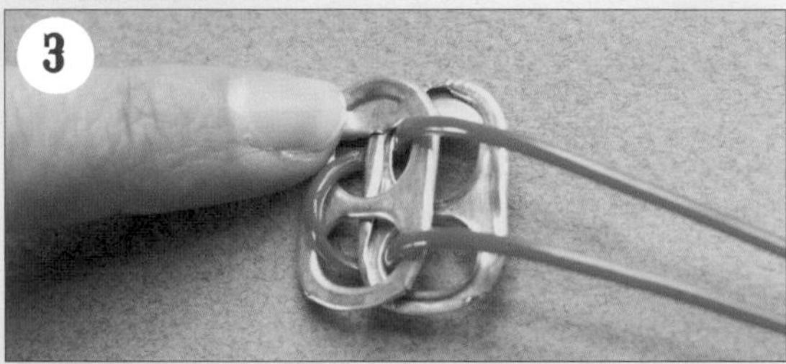

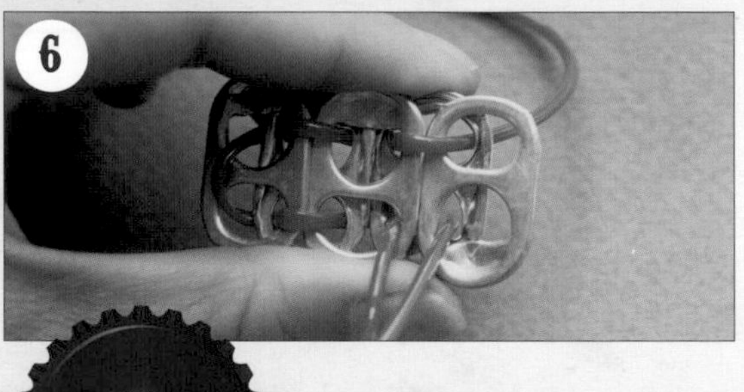

3 Hold a second tab next to the first, slightly overlapping with the rough edges together. Thread the top strand of ribbon through the back of the second tab, then pull the ribbon through the front of both the overlapped holes. Repeat this step, with the bottom strand of the ribbon going around the back of the second tab, up into the overlapped holes in the front.

4 Hold a third tab next to the first with the rough side facing down. Thread the top ribbon into the next overlapped hole, going in from the front and down through the second tab. Repeat this step with the bottom ribbon into the bottom holes, tightening the ribbons as you go.

5 Hold a fourth tab next to the second, rough side facing up. Thread the top ribbon up from the back through the overlapped holes. Repeat with the bottom ribbon.

6 Repeat steps 4 and 5 until your bracelet or belt is the desired length. For a bracelet, thread the ribbon from the last pull tab into the overlapped holes of the first tab, then tie off. For a belt, tie off your ribbon when it's your desired length, using the excess ribbon for tying the belt ends together when you wear it.

Elizabeth Start's Pull-Tab Gown

Cinderella's dress may have come from her bratty sisters' cast-off pearls, hand-me-down fabric, and magic dust, but that's only because there wasn't a six-pack lying around. If her Fairy Godmother were turned loose in the recycle bin after a weekend bender, the results might look something like the stunning pull-tab gown Elizabeth Start constructed.

With a keen eye for design and fashion, Elizabeth has been making clothes and crafts since she was a kid. A self proclaimed "upcycle artist," she's one of those tinkers who exceeds the old silk-purse-from-a-sow's-ear benchmark and would probably construct a set of handbags, travel luggage, and matching shoes if left in a room with those same materials.

Her gown was constructed from approximately seven thousand pull-tabs from cans and took over 250 hours to make. Showcased in the 2007 Trashy Fashion Show, it has also been on display at a number of other fashion and recycled art events.

Elizabeth gathered tabs from family and friends before eventually outsourcing her collection circle to random acquaintances who were happy to donate supplies. Woven together with light blue ribbon, the gown has a sexy slit up the side and a halter-style beaded collar, and it weighs more than thirty pounds.

While Elizabeth's favorite styles of beer are stouts and lagers, she's happiest to partake in a cool Hefeweizen with a lemon wedge. If pressed to pick a favorite material to work with, Elizabeth would choose bicycle parts—especially rubber tires. When she's not working on her shop, **www.restartsomethinggood.com**, Elizabeth can be found behind the counter at SCRAP in Portland, Oregon, where she helps customers, kids, and fellow artists find just the right recycled parts and supplies to magic together their own dream project.

BOTTLE LABEL BELT BUCKLE

I've got a thing for big belt buckles—the kind truck drivers wore when I was a kid. It's a rugged piece of man jewelry that can take a lot of fancifying and still look cool. They look great on gals, too, whether worn on top of a prairie party dress or with your favorite jeans. A number of craft and online stores carry bezel buckle blanks (say that three times fast), which are the perfect size for a favorite label from your collection.

Before starting this project, you'll want to test a spare bottle label. Some take to resin and sealant without the ink bleeding, whereas others may run. Immerse your test label or scrap of label in sealant the night before and let it dry completely. If your design fades or blurs, you can cover your label completely with clear packing tape on both sides before making your buckle. That way, your design will shine through perfectly and be protected, too.

SUPPLIES

- **BEZEL BUCKLE BLANK**
- **SCRAP PAPER**
- **PENCIL**
- **SCISSORS**
- **1 BEER BOTTLE LABEL**
- **GLUE STICK**
- **RESIN EPOXY SEALER OR GLOSSY ACCENTS**
  a clear, dimensional embellishment sealer

How to

1 Lay the buckle blank face down onto a piece of scrap paper and trace around it with a pencil.

2 Flip over the buckle and press the paper inside it, making creases where the excess comes up the sides. Trim the crease marks and check for fit.

3 Use this paper as your template to trace over your beer label.

4 Cut out the label and tack it to the inside of the buckle, using the glue stick.

5 Fill the buckle with sealer and let it dry overnight or as recommended by the manufacturer's instructions.

BEER BOX COWBOY HAT

Perfect for the big game, a day at the races, or hanging out by the river, this cowboy hat is a crowd-pleasing classic. And why is that? Well, pardner, for a couple reasons. First, you're going to need two large beer boxes—one a twelve-count, and the other a twenty-four. That's three dozen beers to share with your friends. On top of that, it's the style statement you'll be making—a symbol of your individuality, and a belief in personal freedom. A cool hat for a cool customer.

SUPPLIES

12-COUNT BEER BOX

RULER

FELT-TIP MARKER

CRAFT KNIFE

SCISSORS

24-COUNT BEER BOX

PHOTOCOPIER

BASEBALL HAT
that fits your head (optional)

SPRAY ADHESIVE

CLEAR PACKING TAPE
(optional)

STAPLER (optional)

12 CANS
24 CANS
24

How to

1 Carefully open the 12-count beer box from the side flap, open a beer, and offer the rest to your pals; you need to empty your box.

2 Open the opposite side of the box and fold the box flat.

3 Measure and mark a line around the box 7 inches from one of the open sides, and use the craft knife to cut all the way around. This will be the top and main part of your hat. Save the other part of the box for another hat.

4 Cut a vertical line across the top of your box and through the top flap. This line should come right between the holes for the handle.

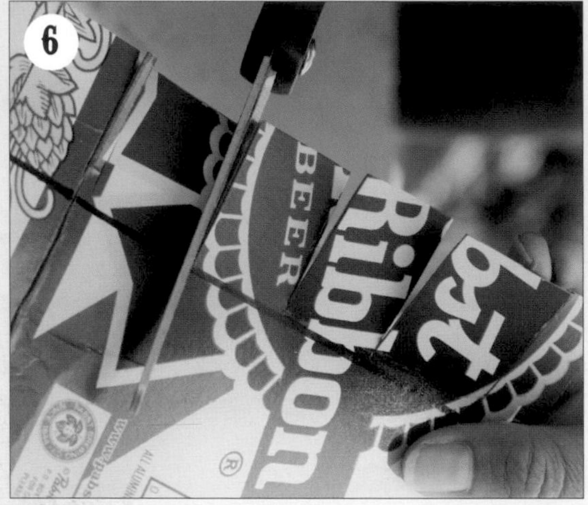

5 Draw a second line all the way around the box, 1 inch up from the line you cut in step 3.

6 Cut slits every inch from the edge you just cut in step 5, around the main part of your hat.

7 Fold the slits away from the hat base.

8 Open the 24-count beer box where the flaps are glued down, being careful not to tear the box or remove any pieces. Refrain from cracking open another cold one. You're about to take some measurements here, so you'll need your wits about you.

9 With right sides out, match the handle holds of the box together and press the box flat, making a fold line across the bottom panel of the box.

10 Use a photocopier to enlarge the pattern on page 27 for the hat crown or use a baseball cap that fits your head perfectly. Place the hat crown pattern or the baseball cap directly in the center of this box, midway between the handle holes and outer edge and trace.

11 Use the craft knife to cut along the crown shape from the hat or the smaller circle from template. Make sure to cut through both layers of the box.

12 Open the box and lay it flat with wrong sides facing you. Working in a well-ventilated space, completely saturate the surface with spray adhesive.

13 Push the main body of the hat through one of the holes, through the label side. You'll need to compress the box top slightly to get it through the hole you may also try unfolding the very top of the hat temporarily if it helps to position the lower part into place. Once the upper part of the hat is all the way through, press the cut tabs down to stick them into the glue.

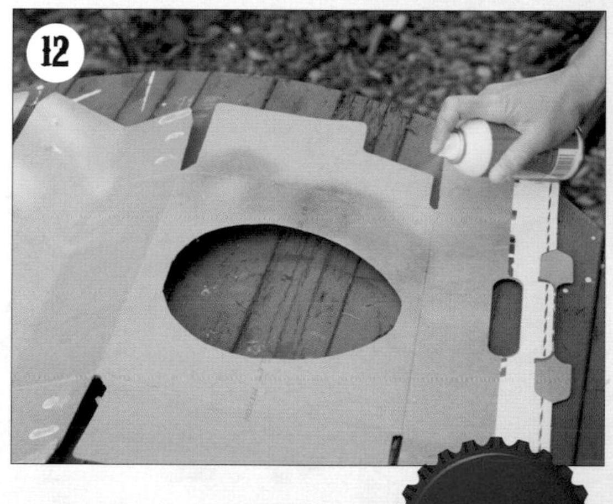

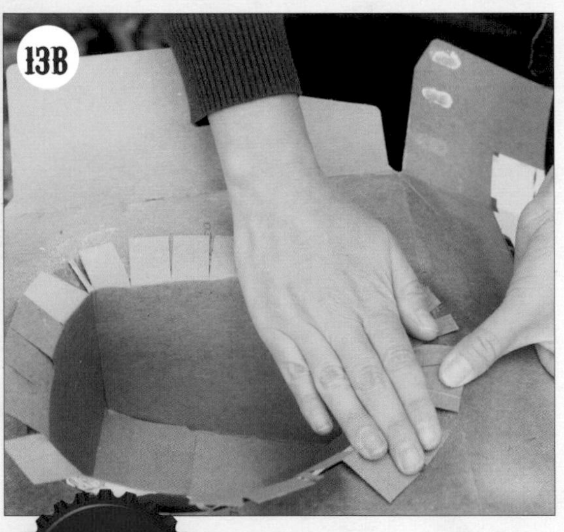

14 Fold the larger box back together so the insides meet.

15 Fold the top flaps of your smaller box back in place, starting with the smaller flaps. Secure them in place on the inside and outside with clear packing tape.

You now have your basic hat shape. To make the outer brim, you can either 1.) cut the larger circle traced from the template, or 2.) while the hat is right side up, eyeball-sketch a large oval shape (1 ½ to 2 inches from the main body piece of your hat) onto the box and cut it out.

16 To add stability to the hat, you can staple the cardboard sections of the hat together, where the brim meets the crown.

17 You may want to cover the outside edges of your brim with packing tape as well, to keep them from coming apart. Cut a 3-inch strip of packing tape and lay it horizontally around the edge of the brim, with half the tape overhanging the edge. Cut slits into the overhanging part of the tape, then fold it over and press it to the underside of the brim.

18 If you want to waterproof your hat, you can cover the rest in packing tape.

Pabst
Blue Ribbon
BEER
IMPORTED BEER
IMPORTED BEER

14
Blue Ribbon
24
CANS

Pabst
Blue Ribbon
12
CANS
Established in
Milwaukee 1844
24/12 FL OZ
CANS
24
CANS

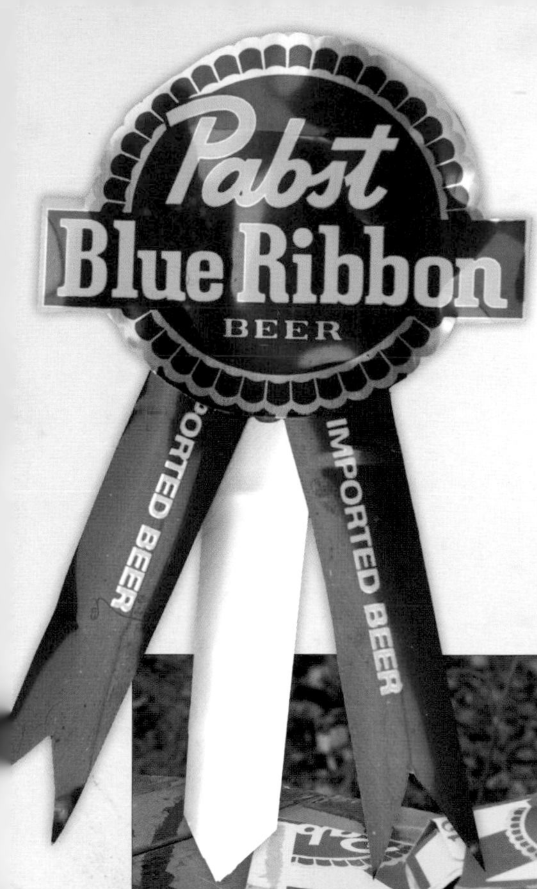

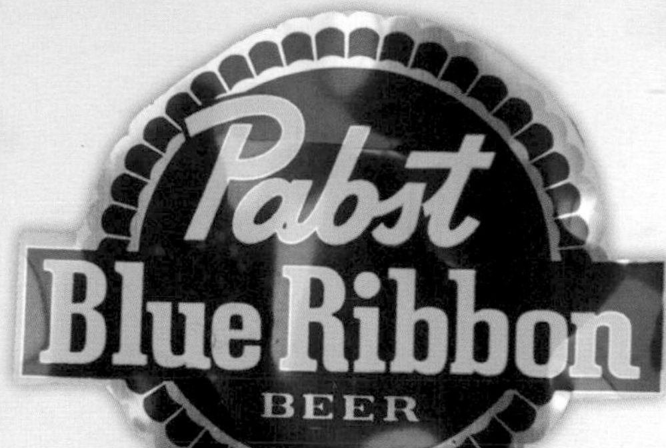

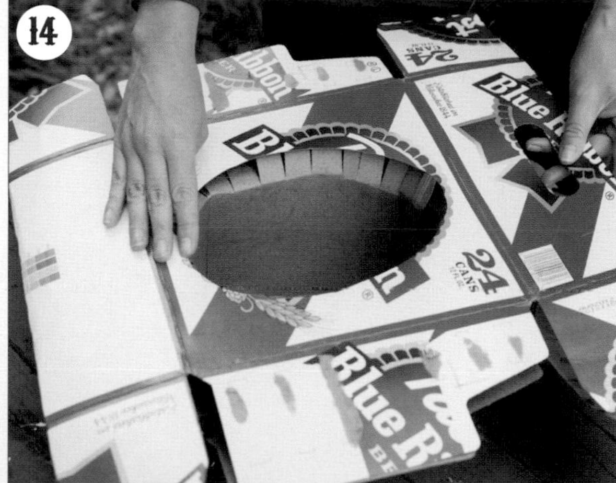

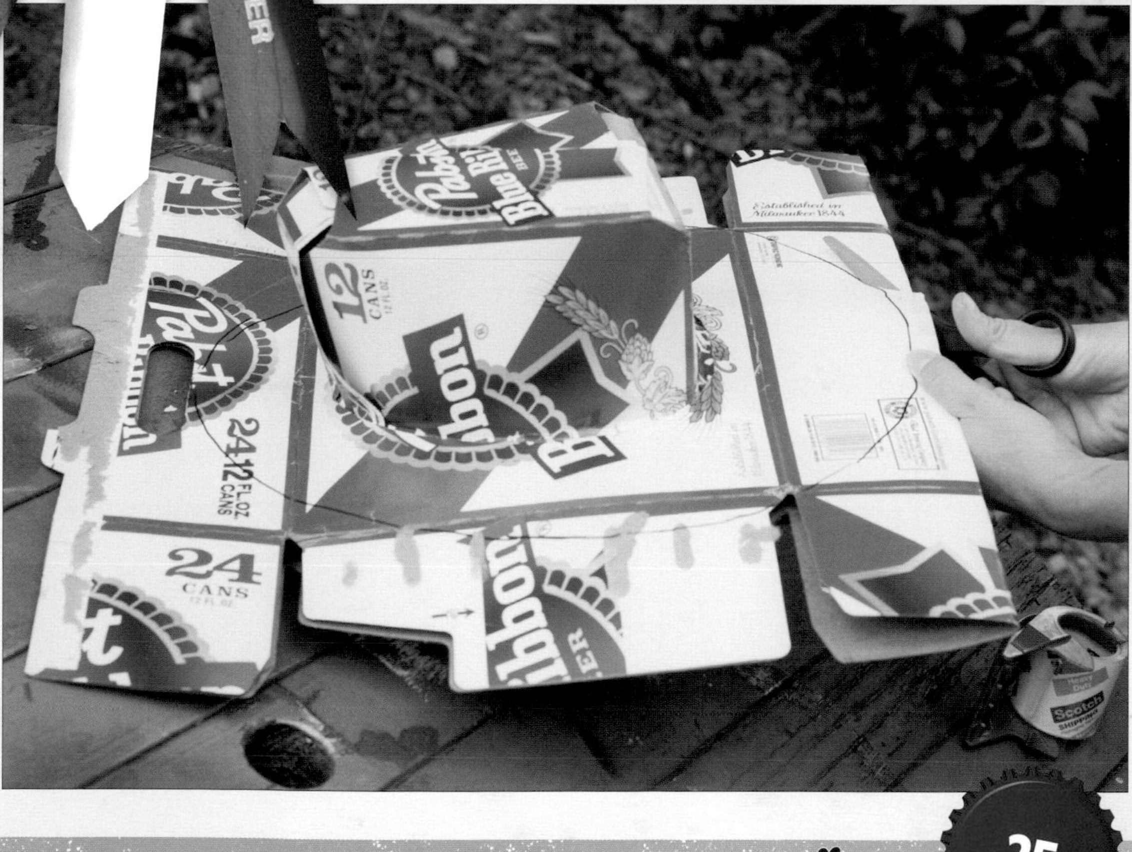

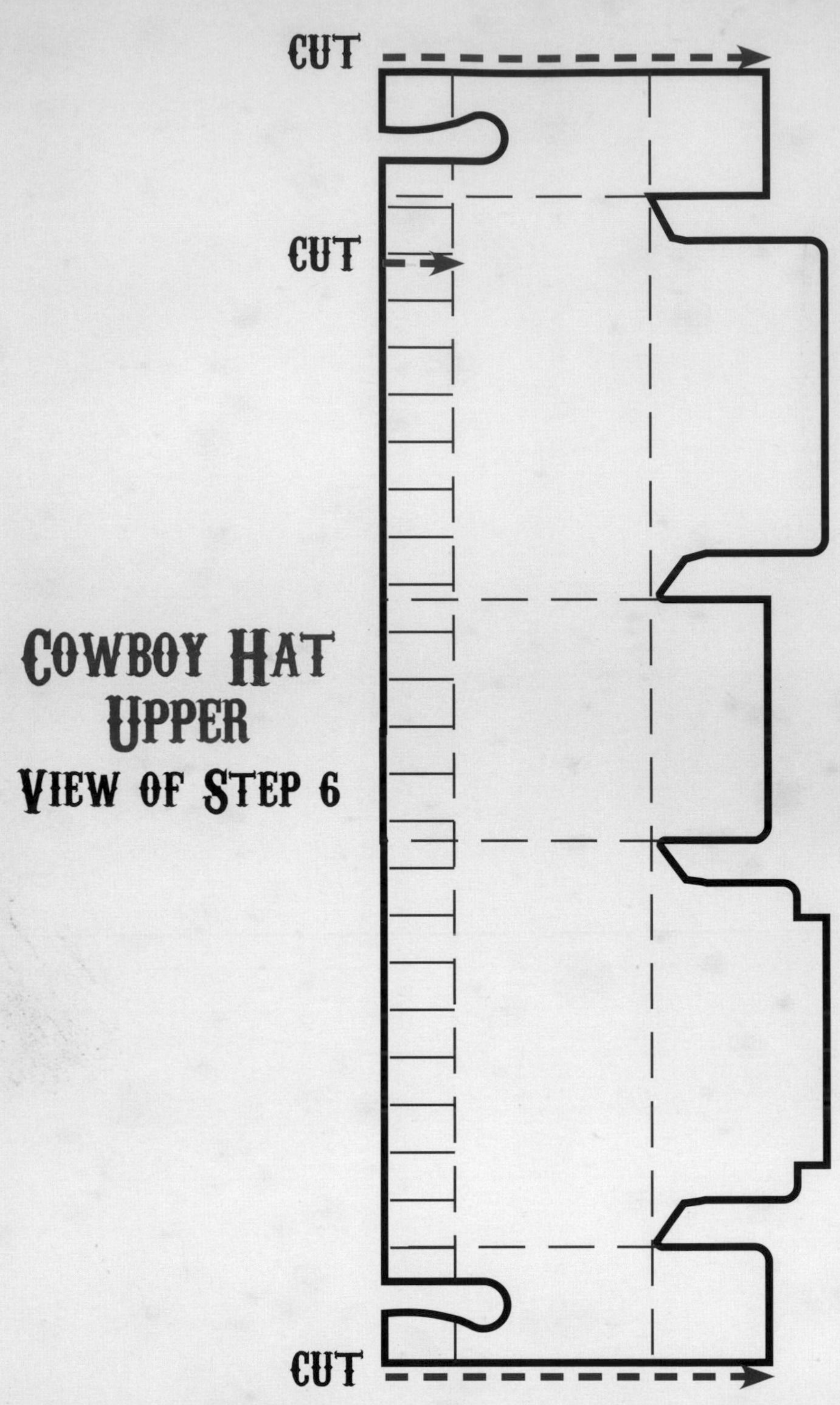

Cowboy Hat Upper

View of Step 6

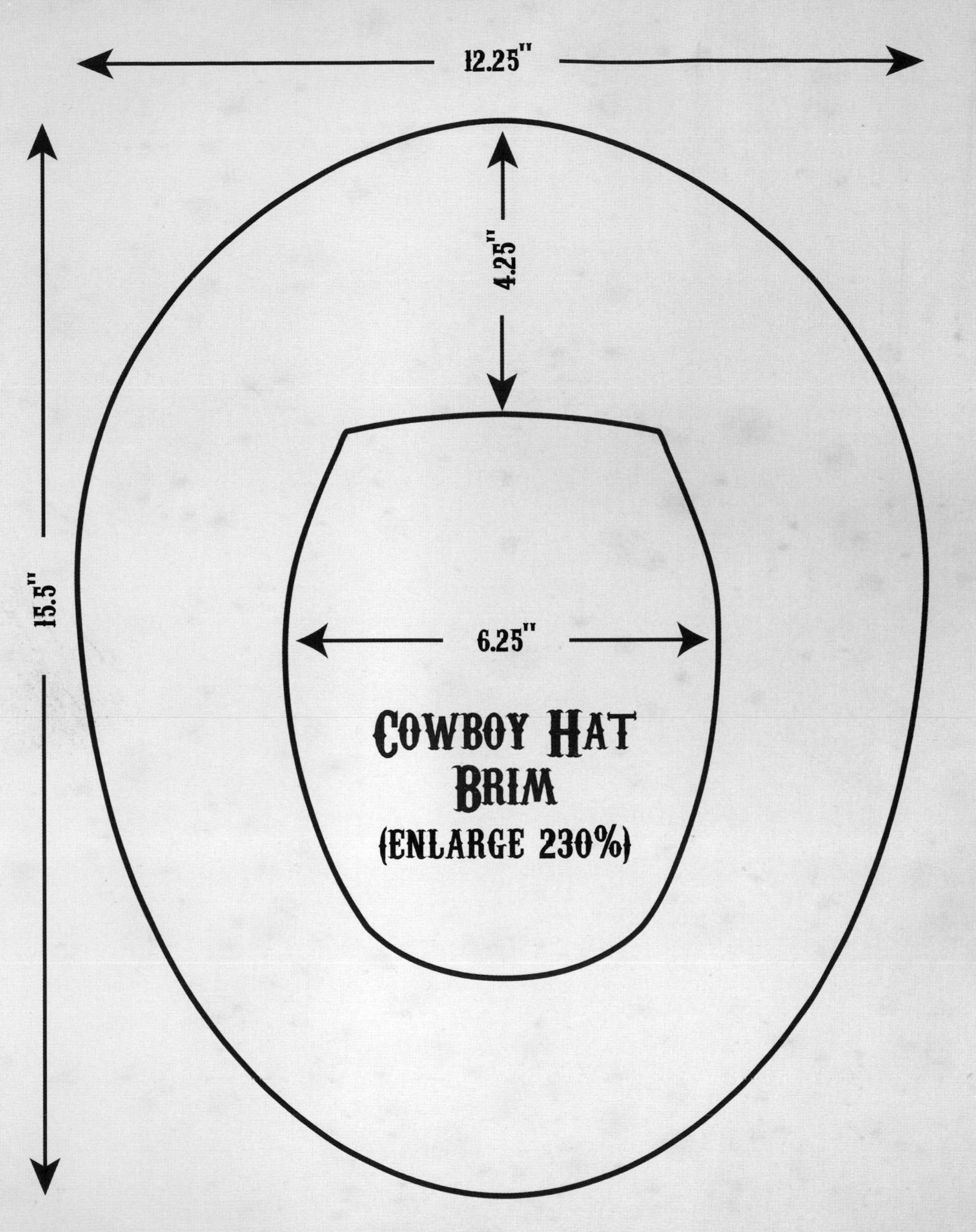
12.25"
4.25"
15.5"
6.25"
COWBOY HAT
BRIM
(ENLARGE 230%)

Bottle Cap Headband

Sometimes, I wear my heart on my sleeve; other times, I shout my love loud and proud from the top of my cranium. Featuring bottle caps on a headband is a fun way to play with colors and patterns while keeping your gorgeous tresses from falling into your beer foam.

Some breweries have only a single signature cap; others have special holiday caps for winter brews, or different colored caps to distinguish brew styles. Of course, you can always spice it up and have a mix of caps from favorite beers, or use a single solid color to match a special outfit.

Supplies

10 BOTTLE CAPS,
or enough to fit your headband

HOT GLUE GUN

WIDE HARD PLASTIC OR METAL HEADBAND

How to

1. Fill the bottle caps with hot glue as described on page xvi and let cool.

2. Glue the caps to the headband.

3. Open a beer and admire your handiwork.

UINTA
BREWING
UINTA
UINTA
BREWING
CO
UINTA

BACK IN THE DAY, THE WORD

THEY WERE THE GO-TO
BEVERAGE FOR HARDWORKING
LADS AND LASSIES.

ALES PACK IN THE
FLAVOR PUNCH AND
QUENCH THE THIRST.

WITH HUNDREDS OF
FOREIGN AND DOMESTIC
BRANDS TO SAMPLE,
YOU'LL HAVE A
CORNUCOPIA OF
CRAFT SUPPLIES
AND INSPIRATIONS
TO CHOOSE FROM.

BEER CAN CANDLE HOLDERS

Perfect for backyard barbecues and romantic evenings at home, these candle holders have a postmodern, industrial look, also known as "bachelor chic" in certain circles. A glam way to upcycle your empties, they can also be used as instant ashtrays for the smoking set.

CANDLE HOLDER 1

1 Use the can opener on the outside of the can to remove the lid.

2 Measure and mark eleven cut lines every ¾ inch around the top of the can. Mark corresponding points around the bottom to act as guides.

3 Use the scissors to cut eleven vertical slits down the length of the can.

4 Place your pencil at the outside edge of the can and roll one flap over it. Continue rolling all the way down until you reach the bottom edge. Repeat for each flap.

SUPPLIES

✻ CANDLE HOLDER 1 OR 2 ✻

CAN OPENER

1 BEER CAN

RULER

PENCIL

SCISSORS

Candle Holder 2

1 Use the can opener on the outside of the lid to remove the top of the can.

2 Measure and mark eleven cut lines every ¾ inch around the top of the can. Mark corresponding points around the bottom to act as guides.

3 Use the scissors to cut eleven vertical slits down the length of the can.

4 Fold out the flaps flat like the petals of a sunflower.

5 Take one flap and fold it over two flaps next to it, about ½ inch from the base.

6 Take the next flap (the first one that you folded the flap on top of) and repeat step 5, folding it onto the next two flaps.

7 Repeat this all the way around your cans, tucking the ends of the previous two flaps underneath the edges that have already been folded.

4

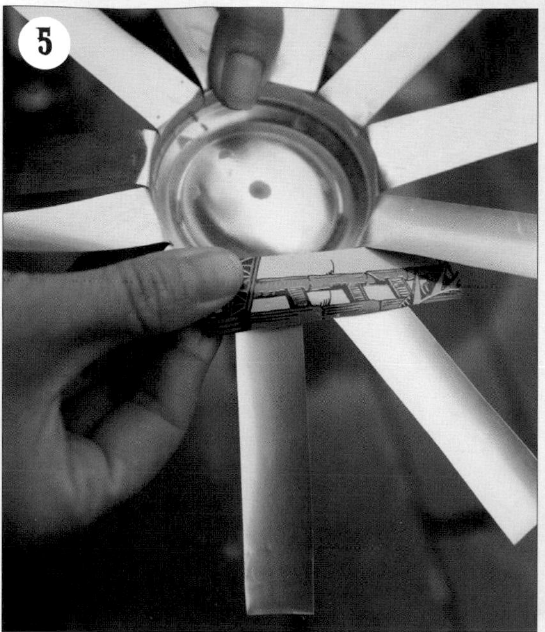
5

6

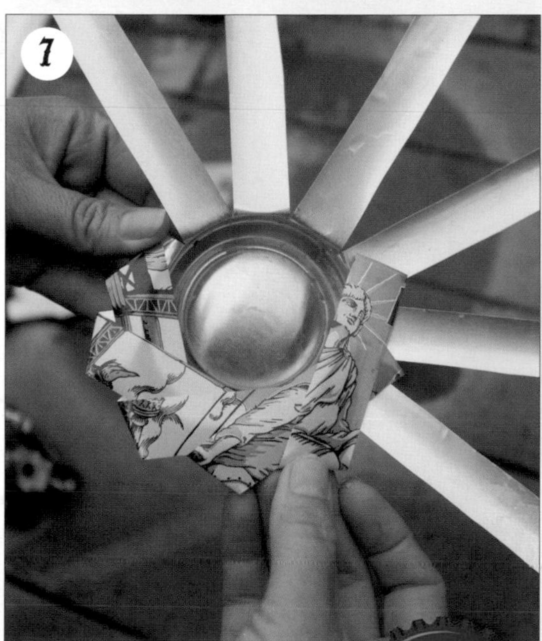
7

BOTTLE CAP CANDLES

While these little cuties might not give enough light to craft by, they certainly set the mood sweetly for other nocturnal hobbies. Bottle cap candles look charming scattered across the picnic table for a dinner al fresco or bundled up with matches in a matchbox and covered in decorative paper as a gift for friends.

Make sure you're using flat caps for this. The bent ones tend to rest at an angle and you could end up with wax all over the place. This is an especially fun way to use up the caps that have something clever written on the inside of the cap.

SUPPLIES

WICK AND METAL WICK BASE (from a candle supply shop)

RULER

SCISSORS

BEESWAX OR OTHER CANDLE WAX BASE, such as paraffin

LARGE KNIFE (optional)

DOUBLE BOILER OR MICROWAVE-SAFE BOWL

BAKING SHEET lined with parchment paper

BOTTLE CAPS

SMALL LADLE

1 Measure and cut a 2-inch strand of wick.

2 Tie a knot in the end of the wick and thread the rest through the wick base.

3 If you're using solid beeswax, use the knife to cut it into 1-inch cubes before melting.

4 Melt the beeswax in the top of a double boiler on low heat or in a microwave-safe bowl for 1 minute on the low setting, or until the wax melts.

5 Place one bottle cap on a lined baking sheet (in case of spills).

6 Place the wick base in the bottom of the cap, wick knot down.

7 Use the small ladle to pour some wax into the cap. It will fill quickly—a little bit goes a long way.

8 Let the wax cool completely before trimming the wick.

9 Repeat with more bottle caps.

10 Take your craft outside, along with a fresh beer. Snuggle your sweetie, and enjoy the magic.

91 92 93
NINKASI BREWING COMPANY
OREGON
12
6
Dark Double Alt
ALE

SIX-PACK CRAFT CADDY

Dang it, if six-pack boxes aren't convenient objects, then I don't know what is. Sure some folks use them just for toting beer, but at my house, they get repurposed to carry all sorts of things: cleaning supplies for the bathroom, assorted ribbons for wrapping presents, and even crafts for the projects in this book. I've put a couple grommet holes in my box to thread my yarn through, it's a handy way to keep small balls from rolling away and keep the yarn separated when making projects that involve multiple colors. I love showing up at picnics with a six-pack in one hand and a caddy filled with yarn, crochet needles, paintbrushes, jars of bottle caps, and scissors in the other. Instant craft party. Bam!

SUPPLIES

1 SIX-PACK BOX

PAPER HOLE PUNCH

GROMMET

GROMMET TOOL

PEN (optional)

HOT GLUE GUN (optional)

BALL OF YARN

CAN OPENER

2 TALL BOY BEER CANS

ELECTRICAL TAPE

1 Open a beer from your six-pack and put the rest in the fridge. You need to make space in your box.

2 Decide what you'll be toting around. For larger objects, you may want to remove one or more of the cardboard bottle separators from the inside.

3 Pick a spot for your grommet and use the hole punch to make a hole. Attach the grommet, using the manufacturer's directions. If you're putting your grommet in an awkward spot, you might want to mark the hole with a pen, gently take apart the box along its glue lines, attach your grommet, then reassemble the box and seal it with hot glue.

4 Stash the ball of yarn in the bottle cubby nearest the grommet, with the end threaded out through the grommet hole.

5 Use the can opener on the inside of a tall boy can to remove the lid. Cover the cut with a piece of electrical tape to keep the can from scraping up your craft tools.

6 Fill the can with art supplies and place in an empty bottle cubby. Repeat with the other tall boy can, placing a pair of scissors in one of the cans, if desired. Place other crafting materials, such as the beer can pincushion (see page 47) in the remaining cubbies. You're good to go!

Bekki Scotto: A Bohemian Mermaid in Humboldt County

Known as "the chick who crochets" in college, fine arts major Bekki Scotto would weld big steel sculptures and crochet onto them, make tiny lace edges on printed photographs, paint giant works out of 1970s crochet pattern books, and blow glass forms specifically to hold crocheted lace covers. With this kind of background it's little wonder that her crocheted beer can hat instructions have become one of the most downloaded patterns of their type on the Internet.

A funky child of the '70s, Bekki grew up learning all types of textile crafts, along with her mom—latch hooking rainbows, crocheting blankets, and cross-stitching jeans. You name it, they embellished it. As an adult, Bekki kept her affinity for the "'70s cheesy craft era," believing that "it was the most fertile time for textile arts and crazy creativity."

With her mantra, "Crochet will save the world!" Bekki is known to show up at parties with yarn and empty and full beer cans, cranking out a stunning hat in an evening as a thank-you gift for hostesses and friends. These days she lives the crafter's dream in Humboldt County, California, where she makes and sells hand dyed clothing on her website **www.bohemianmermaid.com** and at numerous festivals. When she's not busy making, taking her show on the road, or sampling some of her favorite local microbrews, Bekki gives sage advice on her resourceful blog at **www.bohemianmermaid.blogspot.com.**

MANA WHEAT

Bekki's Crocheted Beer Can Sun Hat

When I say the words *beer* and *crafting* to most folks, it is almost guaranteed that a few minutes of our conversation will be devoted to talking about the iconic crocheted beer can hat. Kitschy and eye catching, the beer can hat makes the wearer the fashionable hit of any social gathering. While old-style beer can hats invoke a retro '70s look (and, for some, a shudder of disdain), the patterns in this book make use of natural cotton threads in place of the stiff acrylic Grandma used, and feature the bold graphics of modern can designs. They also have a fresh style. One is a utility-style baseball cap with aluminum brim (page 72), and the one here is a sassy beach hat with a faux basket-weave stitch on the brim.

The hats come together fairly quickly, because the bulk of the real estate is taken up by aluminum rather than yarn. These are easily a weekend project, or an evening one if you're a dedicated hook artist. The cool-looking basket-weave stitch on the brim of this sun hat is a more complicated stitch than beginners may have previously encountered, but it only takes a few minutes to learn, and it is a great motif to use when you need a stiffer fabric.

GAUGE: 4 crochet stitches = 1 inch

FIT: The sun hat fits most head sizes comfortably, assuming an average 24-inch head. To increase the hat size, cut larger beer can panels rather than adjusting the crochet pattern.

SUPPLIES

5 BEER CANS

SCISSORS

PAPER HOLE PUNCH

SIZE H (5 MM) CROCHET HOOK

5 OZ / 142 G / 236 YD / 212 M WORSTED-WEIGHT LION BRAND COTTON YARN IN 157 SUNFLOWER (A)

5 OZ / 142 G / 236 YD / 212 M WORSTED-WEIGHT LION BRAND COTTON YARN IN 136 CLOVE (B), for the trim

2.5 OZ / 70 G / 120 YD / 109 M WORSTED-WEIGHT LILY SUGAR'N CREAM IN 01116 BLUE JEANS (C), for the hat top

1 First, deconstruct your beer cans as described on page xiv. You'll need five aluminum panels, each 3¾ x 3 inches wide. Use scissors to trim the corners to round the edges.

2 With the hole punch, punch out four equidistant holes on the top and bottom of each panel, and five equidistant holes on each side, starting and ending at each corner. You can use the template on page 46.

3 Using the crochet hook and yarn A, sl st into the hole in the top right corner hole of a can, ch 3 (counts as 1 dc), dc 2 into the same hole, dc 3 into the next two holes, dc 5 into the hole at the left corner of the can. Repeat around the can, working 3 dc in the holes along each straight edge and 5 dc in the corners, until you have worked the last 3 dcs and arrive back at the start. Work 2 more dc into the starting corner, sl st into the second ch of the ch 3, and tie off.

4 Repeat this beer can granny stitch on the four other panels.

5 To make the main body of the hat: Place two panel pieces together with the wrong sides facing. With yarn B, insert your crochet hook into the side sts and sc the seams together all the way across. Tie off.

6 Repeat the seam stitching for all the panels, until the hat is joined all the way around.

7 With yarn B, sc an edge around the top and bottom of the main hat body. Counting the top loops, you should have 60 stitches.

8 To make the top of the hat: Starting with yarn B, ch 4. Sl st into the second chain to form a loop.

9 Rnd 1: Ch 3 (counts as first dc here and throughout). Work 9 dc into the ch-4 loop (10 dc total). Sl st into the first dc (third ch of ch 3).

10 Rnd 2: Ch 3, dc into the same st. Work 2 dc into the next st and each st all around. Sl st into the first dc.

11 Rnd 3: Ch 3, dc into the same st and into the next st. *Work 2 dc into the next st. Dc into the next st. Repeat from * around. Sl st into the first dc.

12 Rnd 4: Switch to yarn C. Ch 3, dc into the same st, dc into each of the next 2 sts. *Work 2 dc into the next st, dc into each of the next 2 sts. Repeat from * around. Sl st into the first dc.

13 Rnd 5: Ch 3, dc into the same st, dc into each of the next 3 sts. *Work 2 dc

into the next st, dc into each of the next 3 sts. Repeat from * around. Sl st into the first dc.

14 Rnd 6: Ch 3, 2 dc into the same st, dc into the next 4 sts. *Work 2 dc into the next st, dc into the next 4 sts. Repeat from * around. Sl st into the last dc. Tie off.

You should have 60 stitches around the top of the hat and 60 stitches around the crown. If your count is off, you may add an adjustment row of single crochet stitches, skipping stitches if you are over, or adding stitches if you are under, making sure to spread out the changes along the round so they will be less noticeable. Continue with the pattern as written.

15 Place the hat top along the top edge of the main body, matching up the stitches. With yarn B (starting anywhere), insert your hook into the edge stitches of both pieces and sc the seams together all the way around. Sl st into the starting st and tie off.

16 For the brim: You should have 60 stitches on the bottom edge, ignoring the stitches that join the panels together. Using yarn A, sl st into any stitch.

17 Rnd 1: Ch 3, dc into the same st, dc into each of the next 2 sts. *Work 2 dc into the next st, dc into each of the next 2 sts. Repeat from * around. Sl st into the first dc. (80 sts)

18 Rnd 2: Ch 3, dc into the same st, dc into each of the next 3 sts. *Work 2 dc into the next st, dc into each of the next 3 sts. Repeat from * around. Sl st into the first dc. (100 sts)

19 Rnd 3: Ch 3, work a Front Post Double Crochet (FPdc) as follows: yo, insert the hook behind the post of the next dc from front to back and up again, yo and draw up a loop from behind the post (3 lps on hook), yo and draw through 2 lps, yo and draw through the last 2 lps on hook (one FPdc completed). FPdc around the next dc. Work a Back Post Double Crochet (BPdc) around the next st, similar to the FPdc but inserting the hook from back to front and down again around the post of the dc. BPdc around the next st. *FPdc around each of the next 2 sts, BPdc around each of the next 2 sts. Repeat from * around, ending with 1 BPdc. Sl st to the first ch 3.

20 Rnd 4: Ch3, *BPdc around each of the next 2 st, FPdc around each of the next 2 sts. Repeat from * around, ending with 1 FPdc. Sl st to the first ch3.

21 Rnd 5: Repeat Rnd 4.

22 Rnds 6 and 7: Repeat Rnd 3 twice. Tie off.

CROCHETED SUN HAT 3"X3¾"

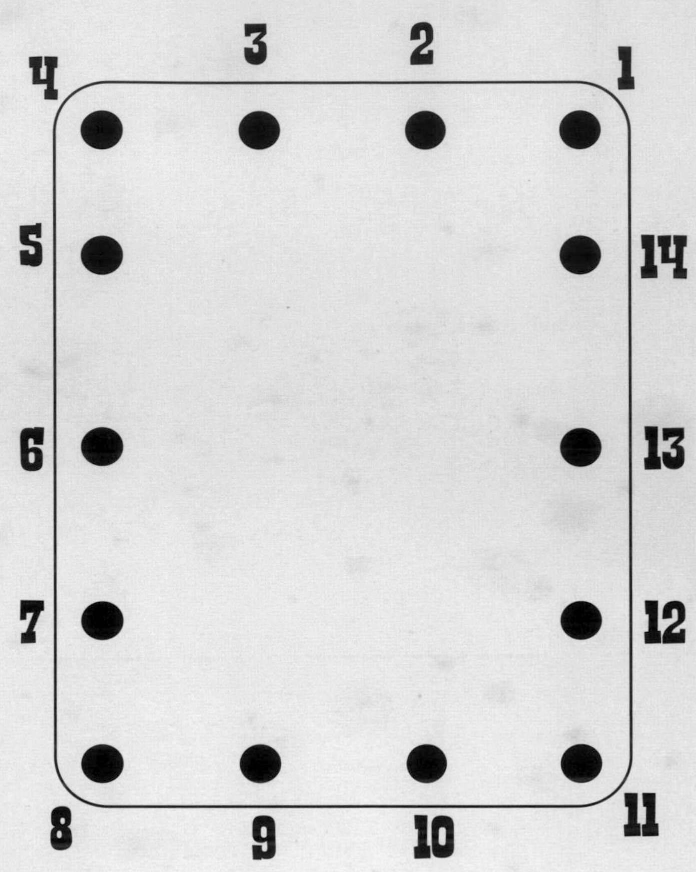

BEER CAN PINCUSHION

This cool project lets you transform your empties into a craft that helps you make more crafts—triple awesome!

Weighted down with small rocks and filled with stuffing, pincushions are inexpensive to make and look super cute when embellished with ribbon and rickrack. This darling upcycle for your notions comes in handy in the sewing room and, of course, fits perfectly into your six-pack craft caddy for on-the-go projects (see page 39).

SUPPLIES

- 1 BEER CAN
- CAN OPENER
- 1 CUP SMALL ROCKS
- SMALL AMOUNT STUFFING OR FIBERFILL (enough to fill the can, plus a generous handful)
- SCISSORS
- 8 X 8-INCH PIECE OF FABRIC
- HOT GLUE GUN
- 12 INCHES OF ANY WIDTH GROSGRAIN RIBBON, for trim
- RICKRACK, BUTTONS, OR SEQUINS FOR EMBELLISHING

1 Open up the can of beer and drain it quickly.

2 Use the can opener to remove the top from the can. Rinse and dry the can, being mindful of the cut edges.

3 Fill the can about halfway with small rocks.

4 Fill the remainder of the can with stuffing, leaving about 2 inches of stuffing coming out of the top of the can. Set aside an extra handful of stuffing for the last step.

5 Cut a 7-inch circle from the fabric.

6 Cut ½-inch slits in fabric every inch all the way around the fabric circle.

7 Hot glue the edge of the fabric to the outside of the can. The slits you cut will help ease the fabric tension, but you'll also want to let the fabric fold onto itself in creases as you glue it down.

8 When you get halfway around the can, insert the rest of the stuffing.

9 Finish gluing the fabric around the can.

10 Put a bead of hot glue around the seam where the fabric meets the can, then place the ribbon on top of the glue beads.

11 Embellish the pincushion ribbon with rickrack, buttons, or sequins.

#9
DRINK•ME
FL OZ (355

Scottish

CUT-CAN JEWELRY

Occasionally I reflect on the famous still from *Breakfast at Tiffany's* in which Audrey Hepburn has that hungry look, peeping though the window at baubles and diadems at the jewelry store. I'm just like that at the beer aisle. Sure, I have a deep longing for the deliciousness inside the cans, but I'm also a sucker for great design, and I absolutely adore some of the innovative and eye-catching art that is going onto my beverages these days. Five minutes with the scissors, small pliers, and some basic jewelry supplies, and blammo, I'm making instant heirlooms.

1 With a can opener on the outside, remove the top of the can.

2 With scissors, cut out your desired design, leaving extra space on top for a jump ring.

3 Use the thumb tack to make a hole for the jump ring.

4 Using pliers or your fingers, open the jump ring and thread it through the can. Close the ring.

5 Thread your chain or earring hook through the jump ring.

SUPPLIES

CAN OPENER

1 BEER CAN

SCISSORS

THUMBTACK

PLIERS (optional)

JUMP RINGS

NECKLACE CHAIN of your desired length, **OR BALL AND COIL EARRING HOOKS**

Beer Can Book Marx

My favorite Groucho Marx quote is: "Outside of a dog, a book is man's best friend. Inside of a dog, it's too dark to read." My dog is a bit of a goofball, so her ranking for my love can vary, but beer and books will always be two of my favorite things, making a great combination. Despite my divided affection, every now and then I have to get serious, put the book away, and give my undivided attention to my drink. I do hate losing my place, though, so I've made these lovely book inserts to mark my territory.

Supplies

1 BEER CAN

SCISSORS

PERMANENT MARKER

CRAFT KNIFE

1 Pick out a fancy beer can and remove the top and bottom.

2 With the scissors, cut down the length of the can to make a flat panel.

3 Cut out your desired shape from the can. Think about making a tall vertical design.

4 Use the marker to draw a large U shape on the back of the piece you cut from your can, and cut along the line with a craft knife.

5 Slide the U shape over your book pages and open a beer.

PYRAMID ALES
need more
— beer

Brew House Message Center and Desk Organizer

Every now and then, I like to bust out a batch of home-brewed beer. Playing with ingredients and brew styles up close and personal has given me a much better insight into what I'm drinking in the bar, and nothing tastes quite as rewarding as a beer you've made yourself.

A good brewer, like a good chef, needs to be organized, with supplies at the ready and ample space to take quick notes during the process. While I designed this note station with a home brewer in mind, it does double duty at my house in the kitchen as a command center for grocery lists (buy more beer) and scheduling playdates. Bonus feature? You get to show off some of the awesome beers that formed your oh-so-clever palate.

Supplies

20 TO 60 BOTTLE CAPS, depending on the size of your dry-erase board

HOT GLUE GUN

MAGNETIZED DRY-ERASE OR CORK BOARD (the one I used for the photo was both)

A TOTAL OF 10 SMALL MAGNETS AND FLAT METAL THUMBTACKS, PLUS 1 SMALL, STRONG MAGNET

CAN OPENER

1 BEER CAN

DUCT TAPE

1 Lay out your caps along the perimeter of the board to see how many you'll need and to determine any pattern you might want to make. Choose ten more caps to ornament the magnets and thumbtacks.

2 Fill all the caps with hot glue and let cool.

3 Glue the board caps to the frame of the board.

4 Glue the magnets and the heads of the thumbtacks to the back of the remaining caps, reserving the one strong magnet for your beer can.

5 Using the can opener on the inside of the lid, cut the top off the beer can and save the pull tab for another project.

6 Line the inside cut of can with tape to keep your pencils from getting scratched.

7 Put the small, strong magnet inside the can and attach the can to the board.

8 Hang the board on the wall and admire your work. Open a beer to celebrate.

Crocheted Beer Can Purse

Like many gals, I'm a fan of accessorizing my outfits, but rather than focusing on style maxims, such as color coordination or not wearing white after Labor Day, I concentrate on matching my ensembles to my moods and to the type of beer I'm up for that afternoon. Some days, I'm a stout girl; other days, I'm a bit bitter. This fetching purse was made from Moose Drool Ale cans, which go with just about anything! I added retro-style bamboo handles to complete the look, and lined the inside with fabric.

GAUGE: 4 crochet stitches = 1 inch

1 First, deconstruct your beer cans as described on page xiv. You'll need ten aluminum panels, each 4 inches tall by 7 inches wide.

2 Trim the can corners slightly to give them rounded edges.

3 Use the hole punch to make four evenly spaced holes on each side of each panel and seven evenly spaced holes across the each top and bottom. You can eyeball it, or copy and cut out the template on page 61 to use as a guide.

4 Using yarn A and the crochet hook, sl st into the hole in the top right corner of a can panel, ch 3 (counts as 1 dc), dc 2 into the same hole, dc 3 into next five holes, dc 3 into the left corner of can. Repeat around the can, working 3 dc in the holes along each straight edge and 5 dc in the corners, until you have worked the last 3 dcs and arrive back at the start.

Supplies

- **10 BEER CANS**
- **SCISSORS**
- **PAPER HOLE PUNCH**
- **PHOTOCOPIER** (optional)
- **14 OZ / 400 G / 710 YD / 655 M WORSTED-WEIGHT BERNAT HANDICRAFTER COTTON YARN IN APPLE (A)**
- **SIZE H (5 MM) CROCHET HOOK**
- **3 OZ / 85 G / 150 YD / 138 M WORSTED-WEIGHT LILY SUGAR'N CREAM YARN IN POWDER 25001 (B)**
- **SAFETY PIN**
- **PURSE HANDLES** (from a craft or sewing store)
- **CARDBOARD FROM A 12- OR 24-COUNT BEER BOX** (optional)
- **FABRIC,** for lining the purse (optional)
- **SEWING MACHINE** (optional)
- **IRON AND IRONING BOARD**
- **NEEDLE AND THREAD** (optional)

POSTAL
MOOSE DROOL
BIG SKY BREWING CO.
MOOSE DROOL
BIG SKY BREWING CO.
MOOSE DROOL
BIG SKY BREWING CO.
MOOSE DROOL
BIG SKY BREWING CO.

Work 2 more dc into the starting corner, sl st into the second ch of the ch 3, and tie off.

5 Repeat this beer can granny stitch on the other nine can panels.

6 Join the panels: Place two panel pieces together with the wrong sides facing. With yarn B, insert your hook into the top left corner and sl st, then sc to end. Without breaking the yarn, take two more can panels and sc a joining seam into these as well. You'll repeat this step for the next six panels, this time with the images of the cans upside down, making sure not to break your yarn. (See the photo for reference.) Once the center seam is finished, you'll want to connect the bottom of the can panels to the top of the ones directly beneath it in a horizontal sc stitch. Repeat this step four times.

7 Make the side panels: Ch 15 and turn. Insert the hook into the second hole from the hook and sc 14. Remember to add a single chain stitch at the end of each row or the beginning of each new row as your turning stitch. Repeat for 32 rows.

8 Attach the side panels: Insert the hook into the top left corner of the side panel and the top right corner of the purse panel. Sc all the way around the seam. The first side will be a little funky, because you're going into the bars between the stitches, rather than into the actual stitches themselves. The easiest way to make sure your work lines up is to safety pin the bottom corners of the side panel into the purse, making sure the stitch holes line up. Repeat this step for the opposite panel.

9 Using yarn B, sc a decorative edge around the top of the purse.

10 Add a fancy handle. I got mine from the craft store and stitched it into place. If you want to really recycle, you could salvage handles from a thrift store bag, or even some old luggage.

At this point, your purse is ready to go, unless you want to go that extra mile and add a lining, which I did, just so I don't lose my laundry money between the crochet stitches at the bottom of the bag.

11 Make the lining: From a flattened empty cardboard beer box, cut out a bottom liner that measures 4½ x 15 inches. Measure and cut fabric for two side panels that are 5 x 10 inches each, two front panels that are 10 x 15½ inches each, and one bottom panel that is 5 x 15½ inches.

12 Sew the front panels to the bottom panel with a ½-inch seam. Press the seam open.

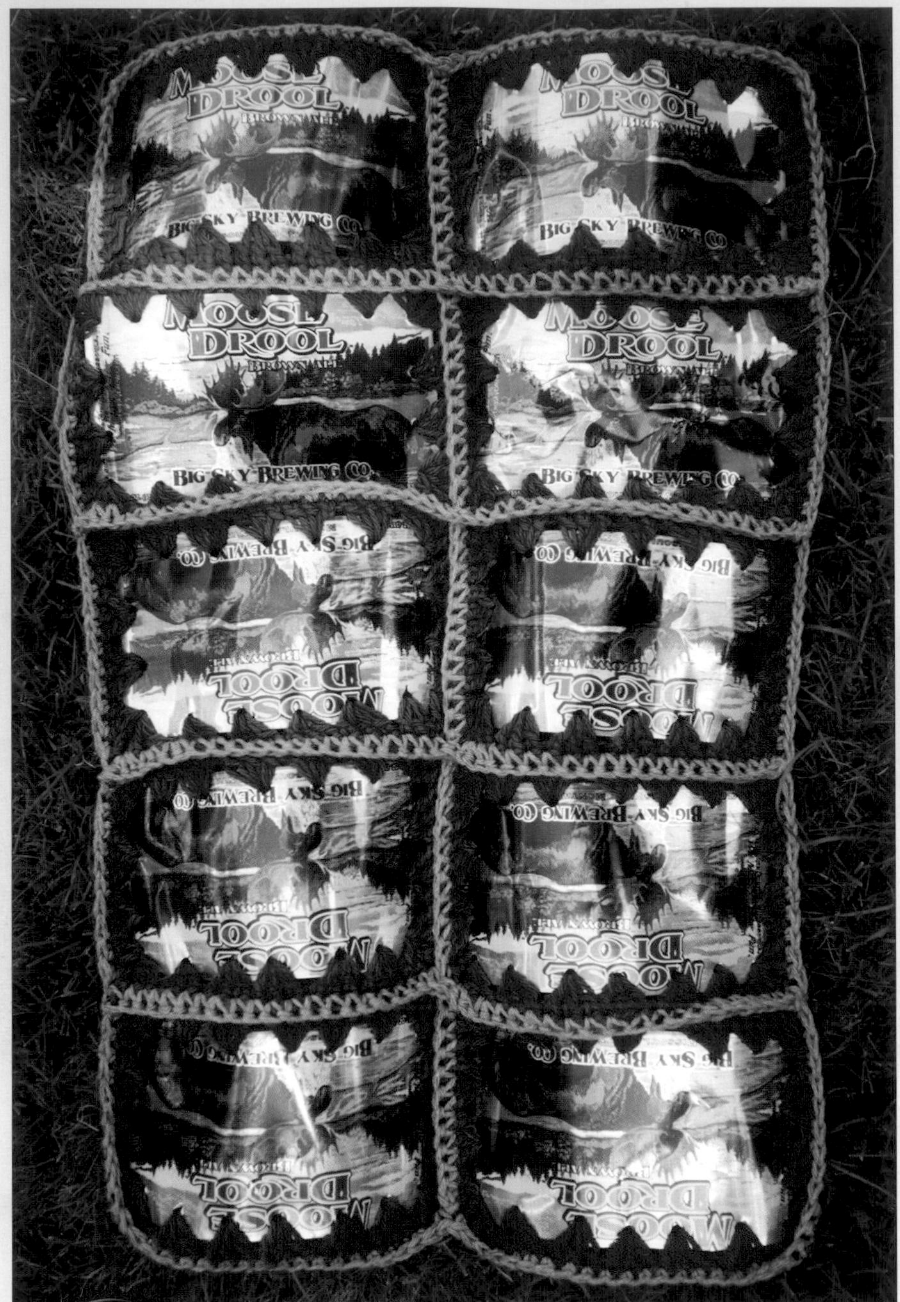

RIGHT SIDE UP

UPSIDE DOWN

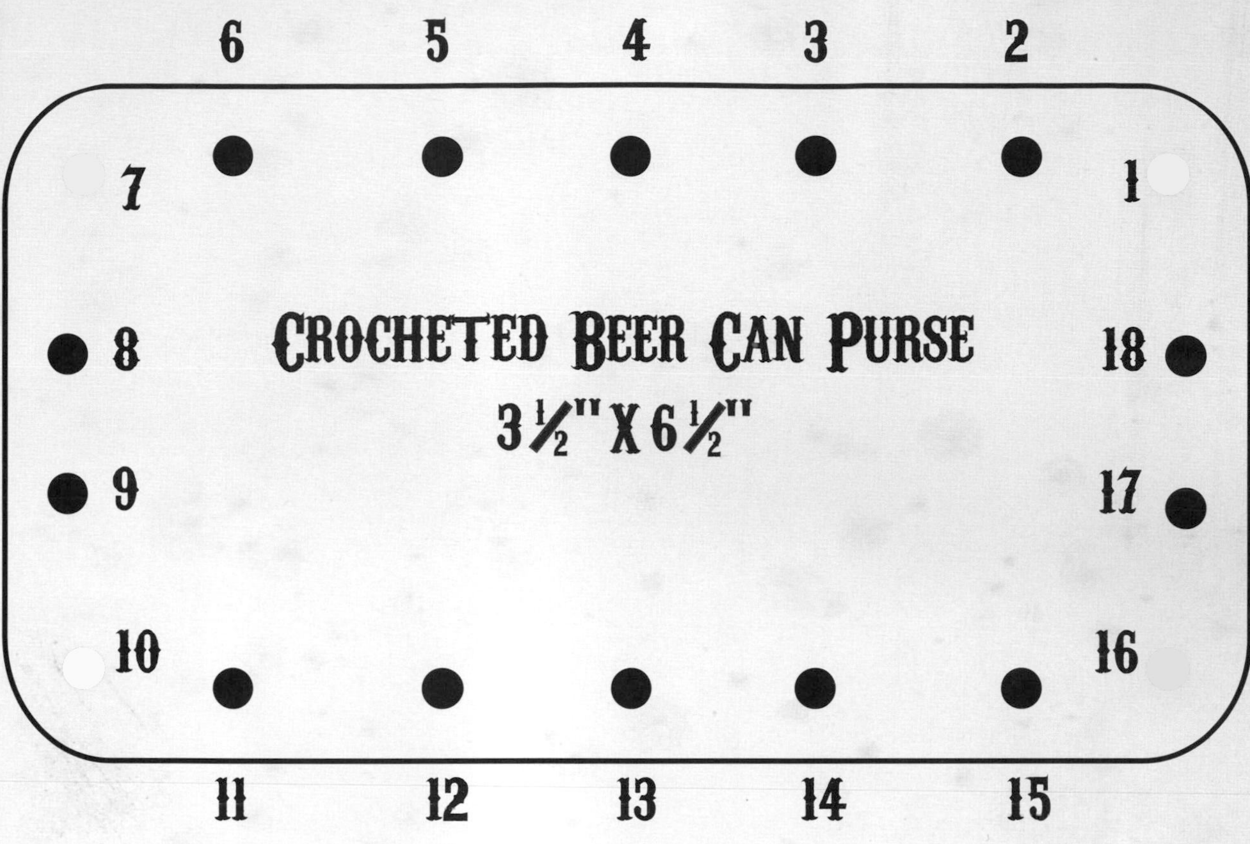

13 Sew the side panels to the front and bottom panels with a ½-inch seam. Cut small notches at the corners, up to about 1/16 inch from the sewing line, to ease the fabric when you turn it.

14 Insert the cardboard liner into the bottom of the purse.

15 Fold down the top of the fabric liner ½ inch, wrong sides together, and press it with a hot iron. Sew around the top of the liner.

16 Turn the lining wrong side out and fit it into the purse. Hand stitch the lining into the purse at the top edge.

BEER CAN PINWHEEL

Sometimes it is the simple things that give us the most pleasure. A warm breeze and a cool brew on a sunny day are the beginnings of a recipe for a blissful moment.

Draining your brewski is the first step in making an awesome toy that makes the most of a gentle wind and your clever crafting skills. Aside from a long corsage pin, which you can pick up at craft stores or florist shops, you've probably got all the supplies you need right at home. If you can't find cocktail straws at the grocery store, your nearest bartender will probably be more than happy to hook you up. (Like you needed the excuse to drop into the neighborhood pub!)

SUPPLIES

PHOTOCOPIER

SCISSORS

TALL BOY BEER CAN

MARKER

PAPER HOLE PUNCH

HAMMER AND NAIL

SPADE BIT from a drill

COCKTAIL STRAW

CORSAGE PIN

LARGE BEAD with a hole big enough for the corsage pin to fit through

NEW PENCIL WITH AN ERASER (preferably unsharpened)

How to

1 Photocopy the template on page 64 and cut it out.

2 Using the scissors, deconstruct the can, removing the top and bottom.

3 Use the marker to trace the template onto the aluminum panel and cut it out.

4 Cut the diagonal lines as marked on the template.

5 Use the hole punch to punch holes in the corners where indicated.

6 Using the hammer and nail, make a hole in the center of your pinwheel and enlarge it by hand, using the spade bit.

OMEN

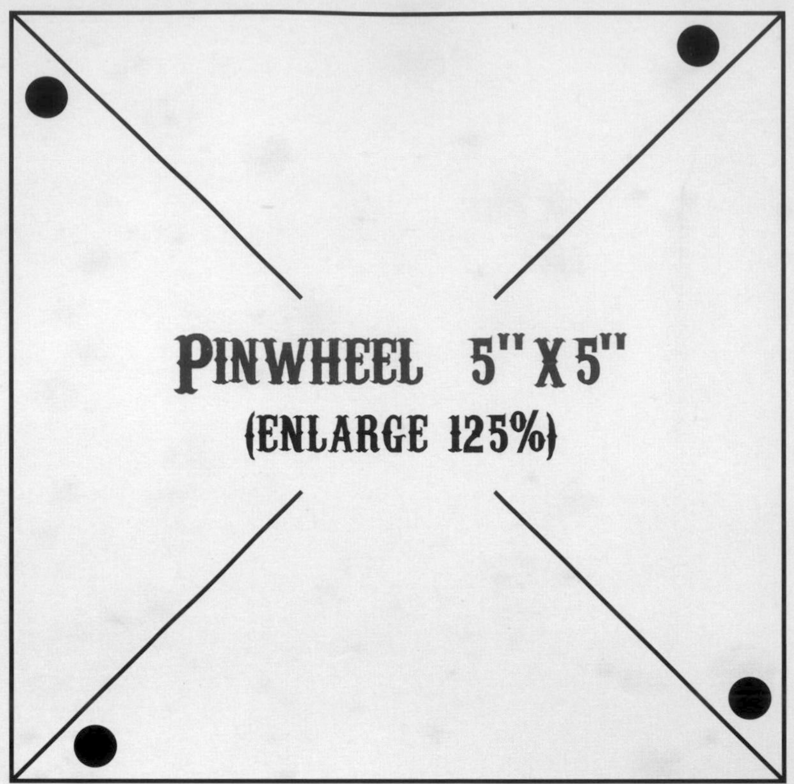

7 Cut the cocktail straw so that it is ¼ inch shorter than the length of the corsage pin.

8 Slide the large bead onto the pin.

9 Thread the corsage pin through one corner of the pinwheel, coming from the label side. Take the next adjacent corner of aluminum and arc it over gently to slide it through its hole onto the pin. Repeat for the two remaining corners. Position the sharp end of the pin so that it fits through the center of the pinwheel.

10 Slide the cocktail straw onto the pin, threading it so it fits through all five holes.

11 Push the sharp end of the pin through the side of the pencil eraser.

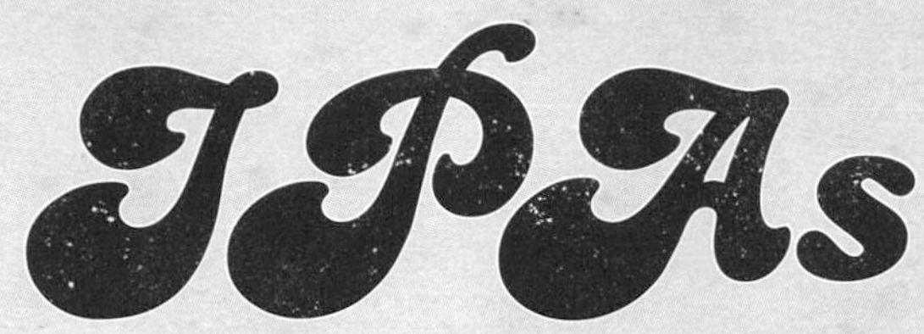

IPAs

PACKED WITH
HOPS
— *and* —
SLIGHTLY BITTER,
IPAS ARE FULL OF
FLAVOR
— *and* —
SLIGHTLY SWEET.

WHEN THE HOPS
START TO FLOWER,
IT'S TIME TO BASK
IN NATURE'S BOUNTY,
AND THESE ARE THE
PERFECT
BEER
CRAFTS
TO ENJOY OUTSIDE.

ATHERLITE
INTERIOR
Full Sail

FLOWER CAP FLIP-FLOPS

When summer time rolls around, there is nothing I like more that cracking a cold one by the pool and giving my little piggies some fresh air. My flip-flops see a lot of wear, and rather than pitch them out when they get to looking shabby, I like to give them a face-lift. Fake fabric flowers from the thrift store and a bottle cap center are the perfect upcycle to refresh my waterside wardrobe. Steer clear of the plastic flowers, they don't take to the hot glue well, becoming melty and distorted.

1 Fill the caps with hot glue and let cool.

2 Your flowers will probably have some type of plastic base to them, and a plastic center part holding the flower together. Remove the flowers from the stems and take them completely apart.

3 Cut a small circle of felt about the size of a half-dollar. You don't need to be too precise on this because the felt will be hidden under your flower.

SUPPLIES

HOT GLUE GUN

2 BOTTLE CAPS

2 FAKE FLOWERS
made of fabric

1 PAIR FLIP-FLOPS

SCISSORS

1 SMALL SHEET OF FELT

4 Position the felt on the inside of your flip-flop, where you'd like your flower cap arrangement. Hot glue into place.

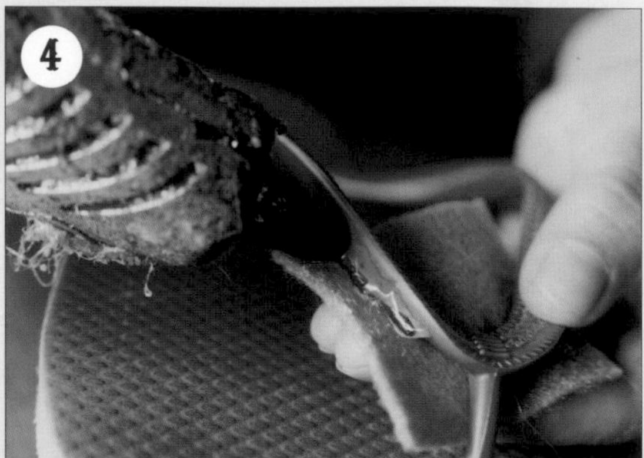

5 Glue your flower to the top of the shoe, onto the felt. With your flower disassembled, you may need to glue each petal layer in place individually.

6 Glue the bottle cap to the center of the flower.

7 Open a fresh beer and admire your hard work.

BEER CAN LANTERN

An awesome craft for hot summer evenings, empty cans are filled with water and frozen overnight. The ice inside the can keeps it from denting when you punch in your design, using a thumbtack or small nail. When all the work is done, let the ice melt out and drop a candle inside to illuminate your awesomeness. You can either use the template provided or trace your own illustration onto your can to make a glowing masterpiece.

SUPPLIES

1 BEER CAN

CAN OPENER

PAPER HOLE PUNCH

1 SMALL TOWEL

1 THUMBTACK OR SMALL NAIL

18-INCH LENGTH OF WIRE, for hanging the lantern

PLIERS

TEA LIGHT OR VOTIVE CANDLE

1 Open a beer and empty the can.

2 With the can opener on the inside of the lid, then remove the top of the can.

3 Use the hole punch to make two holes on opposite sides of the can for attaching the hanging wire.

4 Fill the can three-quarters of the way full with water. Don't fill it to the top, or your can will explode.

5 Place the can in the freezer for several hours, until frozen solid.

6 Lay the can on its side on top of a towel. Following the illustration provided, or your own design, make holes with a thumbtack or small nail, following the punch marks. You can tape the illustration to the can to make it easier.

7 Let the ice melt, then dry the can.

HOP FREAKS UNITE!
BREWING CO
DIA PALE ALE
AVERY BREWING
EST. 1993
BOULDER, CO
6.5% ALC/VOL

BEER

8 Thread one end of the wire through one of the two holes you punched in the top of the can. Use the pliers to twist and secure the end. Thread the other end of the wire through the other hanging hole and use the pliers to twist and secure the end.

9 Drop the tea light or votive candle inside. If some of your holes aren't large enough, blow out the candle and insert a slightly larger nail into the holes.

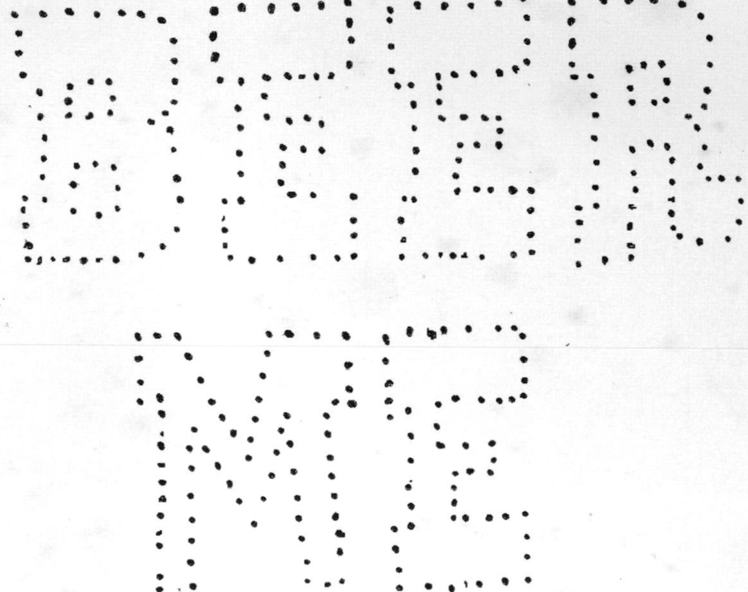

BEKKI'S CROCHETED BEER CAN BASEBALL CAP

More practical than bell-bottom jeans, and more high tech than an eight-track player, beer cans are a sweet blast from our past making a big comeback—and they're better than ever.

Unlike bottles, cans keep all the light out and seal in the oxygen, giving beer that creamy, straight-from-a-keg taste, and new polymer coatings on the inside of many cans act as a barrier from the aluminum, so there are no metal flavors either. For many breweries, especially small start-up companies, cans are the most economical choice for getting new premium beers into stores. Mobile canning companies even come to them on packaging day so they don't have to set up their own expensive production lines or ship the beer out.

How does this translate to the savvy beer crafter? Not only do you get a huge variety of new beers to sample in cans, from watermelon wheats to full-bodied Imperial stouts, but you also get bold packaging designs and an abundant supply of colorful aluminum to choose from.

Taking its cue from the beer can revolution, this crocheted baseball hat is updated, too. It uses cotton yarn and an aluminum visor, and it's completed with a row of crochet under the brim for support and style points, keeping the sun out of your eyes, and you cool inside, just like that brewski in your hand.

GAUGE: 4 crochet stitches = 1 inch

FIT: The cap fits most head sizes comfortably, assuming an average 24-inch head. Rather than adjusting your crochet pattern for a larger head size, you can always cut your beer cans slightly wider.

SUPPLIES

SCISSORS

6 BEER CANS

PAPER HOLE PUNCH

SIZE H (5 MM) CROCHET HOOK

5 OZ / 142 G / 236 YD / 212 M WORSTED-WEIGHT LION BRAND COTTON YARN IN 152 ESPRESSO

PHOTOCOPIER

FELT-TIP MARKER

NEW BELGIUM
BREWING
RANGER
INDIA PALE ALE

How to

1 First, use the scissors to deconstruct your beer cans by removing their top and bottom, then cutting five aluminum panels, 3½ x 3½ inches wide each, and one panel that is 7½ inches wide to make the brim. Use scissors to trim the corners to round the edges.

2 With the hole punch, punch out four equidistant holes on the top and bottom of one panel and five on each side. (See page 76.) Repeat with the four similar panels.

3 Using the crochet hook and the yarn, sl st into the hole in the top right corner of a can, ch 3 (counts as 1 dc), dc 2 into the same hole, dc 3 into the next two holes, dc 5 into the left corner of the can. Repeat around the can, working 3 dc in the holes along each straight edge and 5 dc in the corners until you have worked the last 3 dcs and arrive back at the start. Work 2 more dc into the starting corner, sl st into second ch of the ch 3, and tie off.

4 Repeat this beer can granny stitch on the four other panels.

5 To make the main body of the hat: Place two panel pieces together with the wrong sides facing. Insert your crochet hook into the side sts and sc the seams together all the way across. Tie off.

6 Repeat the seam stitching for all the remaining panels, until the hat is joined all the way around.

7 To make the top of the hat: Ch 4. Sl st into the first chain to form a loop.

8 Rnd 1: Ch 3 (counts as first dc here and throughout). Work 9 dc into the ch-4 loop (10 dc total). Sl st into the first dc (third ch of ch 3).

9 Rnd 2: Ch 3, dc into the same st. Work 2 dc into the next st and each st around. Sl st into the first dc.

10 Rnd 3: Ch 3, dc into the same st and into the next st. *Work 2 dc into the next st. Dc into the next st. Repeat from * around. Sl st into the first dc.

11 Rnd 4: Ch 3, dc into the same st, dc into each of the next 2 sts. *Work 2 dc into the next st, dc into each of the next 2 sts. Repeat from * around. Sl st into the first dc.

12 Rnd 5: Ch3, dc into the same st, dc into each of the next 3 sts. *Work 2 dc into the next st, dc into each of the next 3 sts. Repeat from * around. Sl st into the first dc.

13 Rnd 6: Ch3, 2 dc into the same st, dc into the next 4 sts. *Work 2 dc into the next st, dc into the next 4 sts. Repeat from * around. Sl st into the last dc. Tie off.

You should have 60 stitches around the top of the hat and 60 stitches around the crown. If your count is off, you may add an adjustment row of single crochet stitches. Make adjustments by skipping stitches if you are over, or adding stitches if you are under, making sure to spread out the changes along the round so they will be less noticeable. Continue with the pattern as written.

14 Place the hat top along the top edge of the main body, matching up the stitches. Insert your hook into the edge stitches of both pieces and sc the seams together all the way around. Sl st into the starting st and tie off.

15 To make the brim: Copy the brim pattern (page 77). Cut out the pattern and use the marker to trace it onto the flattened beer can brim panel. Use the hole punch to add holes as shown in the illustration.

16 Crochet as for the other panels, with 5 dc into the corners and 3 dc into all other holes.

17 With right sides facing, line up the brim where you want it. Rather than joining the brim at the bottom edge, you may want instead to attach it higher into the hat body, into the lower granny stitches. This will help your brim face forward, baseball cap style, rather than point straight down. Sl st into the corner st of the brim and join to the hat edge using sc stitches all the way across. Tie off.

BASEBALL CAP 3½" X 3½"

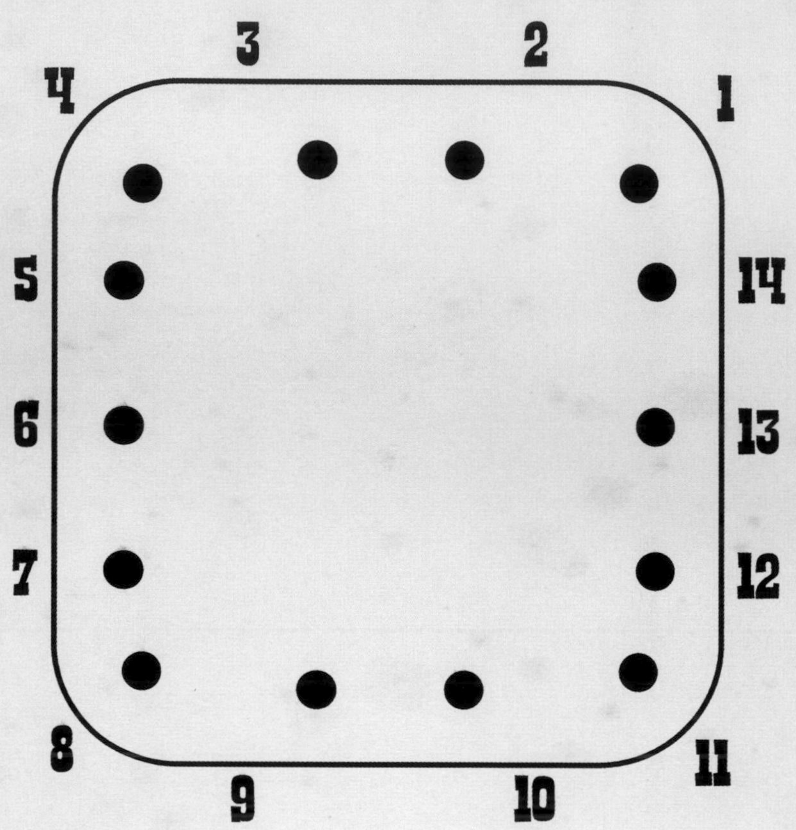

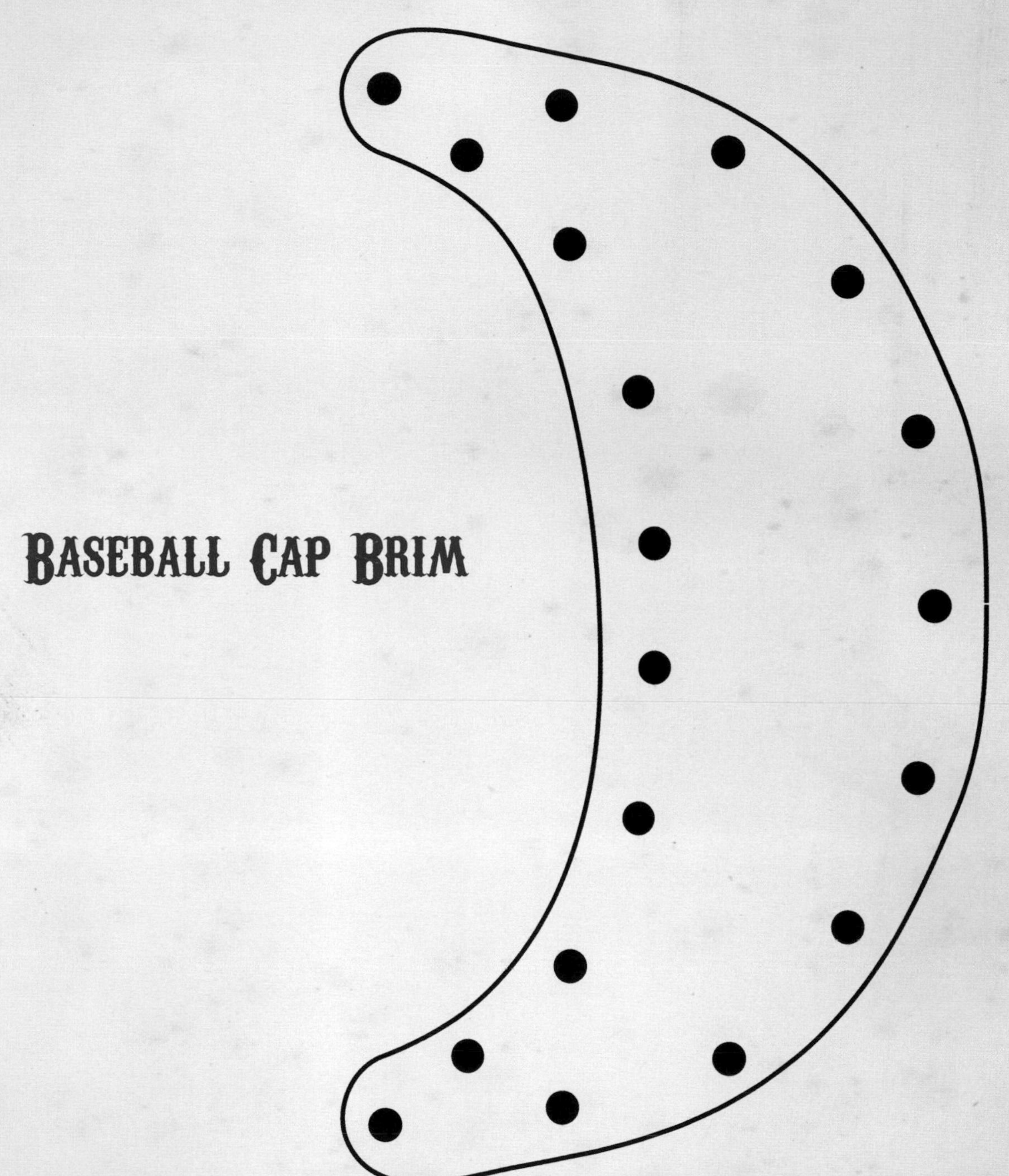
BASEBALL CAP BRIM

RANGER
RANGER
RANGER
RANGER
RANGER

Crocheted Beer Can Dog Jacket

When they talk about man's best friend (ahem, and women's, too) most folks are referring to their pooch, and I suppose I am, too, though a cold six-pack runs a close second. The winning answer would be a dog who can fetch my beer. My dog is loyal but not that smart, and she's got pretty short hair that leaves her shivering in our cold, rainy winters. To keep her cozy, I crocheted her this stunning jacket that matches my fetching Baseball Cap (page 72). She might not bring me my beer, but at least she'll look good wearing it.

Sierra is a medium-size dog weighing in around thirty pounds and standing twenty-one inches at the shoulders, with a twenty-seven-inch waist. Depending on the size of your canine pal, you may want to adjust the pattern.

Supplies

SCISSORS

15 BEER CANS

PAPER HOLE PUNCH

SIZE H (5 MM) CROCHET HOOK

5 OZ / 142 G / 236 YD / 212 M WORSTED-WEIGHT LION BRAND COTTON YARN IN 134 AVOCADO (A)

5 OZ / 142 G / 236 YD / 212 M WORSTED-WEIGHT LION BRAND COTTON YARN IN 152 ESPRESSO (B)

SAFETY PINS

FELT-TIP MARKER

2 BOTTLE CAPS

HOT GLUE GUN

2 SHANK BUTTONS (the kinds with a loop in the back for sewing on)

SMALL NAIL (optional)

NEEDLE AND HEAVY THREAD

GAUGE: 4 crochet stitches = 1 inch

How to

1 First, use the scissors to deconstruct the beer cans as described on page xiv. You'll need fifteen panels, each 3½ x 3 inches wide. Throw your dog a bone while you're at it, as this might take a while.

2 Use the scissors to trim the can corners slightly to give them a round edge.

3 With the hole punch, punch out four equidistant holes on the top and bottom of each panel and five holes on each side.

4 Using the crochet hook and yarn A, sl st into the hole in the top right corner of a can, ch 3 (counts as 1 dc), dc 2 into the same hole, dc 3 into the next two holes, dc 5 into the left corner of the can. Repeat around the can, working 3 dc in the holes along each straight edge and 5 dc in the corners, until you have worked the last 3 dcs and arrive back at the start. Work 2 more dc into the starting corner, sl st into the second ch of the ch 3, and tie off.

5 Repeat this beer can granny stitch on the other fourteen can panels.

6 To join the panels: Place two panel pieces together with the wrong sides facing. Using yarn B, insert your hook into the top left corner and sl st, then sc all the way across. Tie off. Repeat with three more panels to make the first row.

7 Make a second and third row of panels as described in step 6.

8 Attach all three rows together at the top and bottom of the panel, using sc stitch.

9 You should now have a 14½ x 23-inch blanket of squares.

10 With yarn B, sl st in any hole on the outside of the jacket and ch 3, then dc into next hole and the rest of the holes all the way around until you return to beginning. Sl st into the ch 3 and tie off.

11 Make the tummy strap: Ch 12 using yarn A.

12 Rnd 2: Sc into the second stitch from hook and next 10 sts to the end of the row. As you are turning, remember to add a single chain stitch at the end of each row or the beginning of each new row.

13 Continue until the strap is the desired length for your dog. My pattern measures 13½ inches.

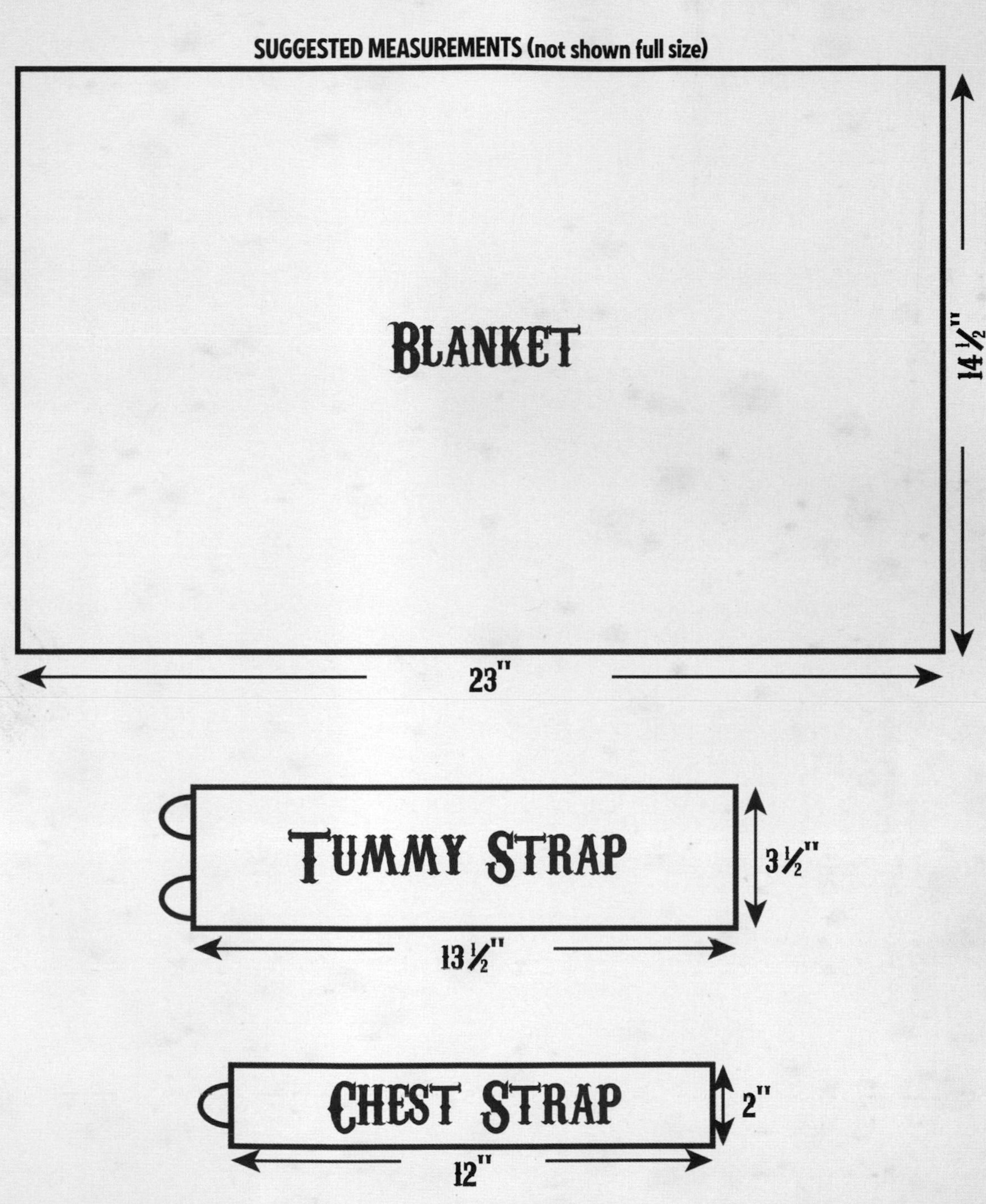
SUGGESTED MEASUREMENTS (not shown full size)
Blanket
14 ½"
23"
Tummy Strap
3 ½"
13 ½"
Chest Strap
2"
12"

14 Using yarn B, sc around the top (long edge), right (short edge), and bottom (long edge) of the strap. On the left (short edge) of the strap, sc into the first hole, ch 8, skip two holes, sc 3, ch 8, sc, and sl st into the first sc of the contrast row. Tie off.

15 Make the chest strap: Using yarn A, ch 7.

16 Rnd 2: Sc into the second st from the hook and next 5 sts to the end of the row. As you are turning, remember to add a single chain stitch at the end of each row or the beginning of each new row.

17 Continue until the strap is the desired length for your dog. My pattern measures 12 inches.

18 Using yarn B, sc around the top (long edge), right (short edge), and bottom (long edge) of the strap. On the left (short edge) of the strap, sc 2, ch 6, skip one stitch, sc2, and sl st into the first sc of the contrast row. Tie off.

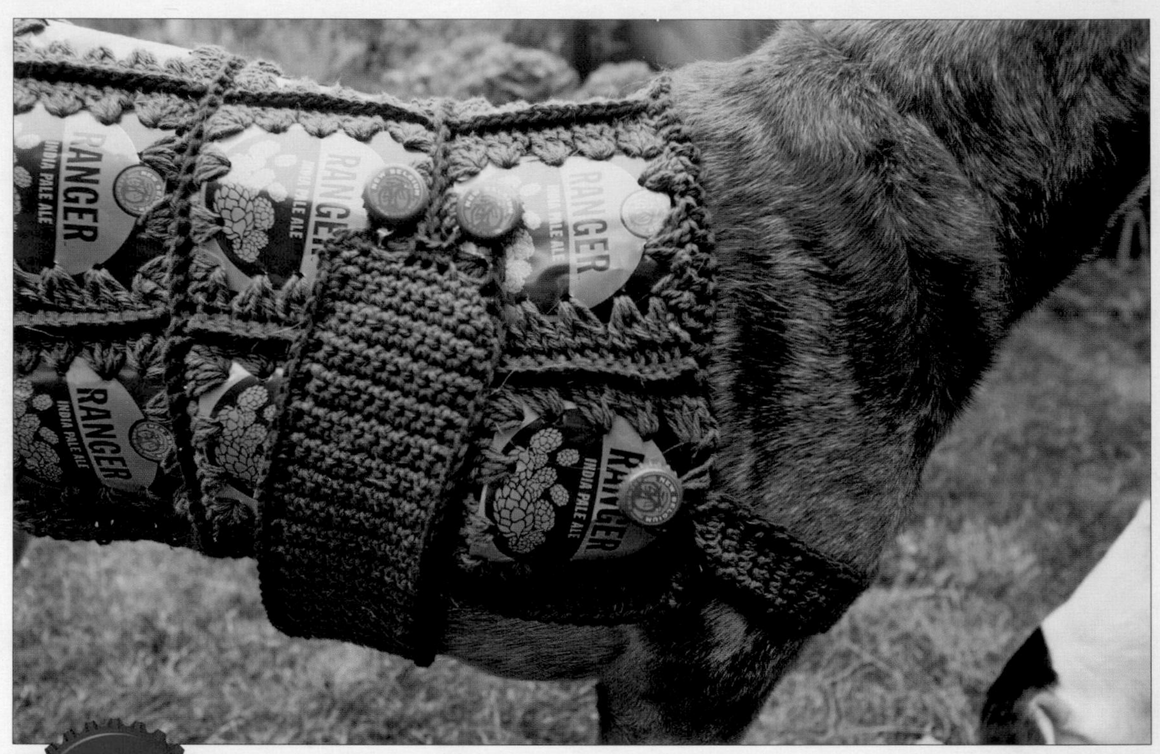

19 Position the jacket on your dog and check the strap fit. The tummy strap should fit underneath just behind the front legs. Use a safety pin on the left-facing edge to hold it in place temporarily. Use the marker to mark (on the right-facing side) where on the cans the buttons should be placed. In a similar fashion, check the chest strap. It should ride in the middle of the chest area, well beneath the dog's throat. Temporarily secure it with a safety pin on the left-facing side and mark the button placement on the right-facing side.

20 Attach the straps to the jacket on the left sides, using sc stitch into the back of the loops.

21 Make the buttons: Fill the bottle caps three-quarters of the way with hot glue and let cool. Add a bit more glue and place the buttons front side down in the hot glue. Let cool.

22 Attach the buttons: Find your marked points. If they're on aluminum, pierce the can with small nail and push the button shank through to the other side. Use the needle and heavy thread to sew the button loop to the nearest yarn. Use a little hot glue to seal it. If the button is to be placed over the crocheted area, simply sew in place.

DALE'S
PALE ALE

Beer Can Fishing Tackle

Fishing and beer are natural BFFs. I really can't imagine enjoying one without the other in the summertime. And what could be more satisfying than catching a fish with a spinner you fashioned yourself from beer can and bottle empties? Fish love reflective and shiny surfaces like what you'd find on the inside of any can, and stripes and patterns remind them of tasty smaller prey they like to feed upon. Sure to appeal to lake loungers in your life, fishing spinners in Dad's favorite brand make an excellent Father's Day gift.

Crafters can raid their jewelry stash to make most of the tackle shown here, or you can head over to your favorite sporting goods store for supplies. They should have the looped wire shaft, fishing lure weights, split rings, clevis, barrel swivel, fishhook, and plastic bait.

Supplies

- **SCISSORS** (for Lure 1)
- **BEER CAN** (for Lure 1) **OR BOTTLE CAP** (for Lure 2)
- **HAMMER AND NAIL** (for Lure 1)
- **LOOPED WIRE SHAFT, OR 8 INCHES OF HEAVY CRAFT WIRE** with a small, strongly secured loop at one end (for Lure 1)
- **PLASTIC SQUID** or other fish bling
- **BEADS**
- **CLEVIS** to fit your wire
- **WIRE CUTTERS**
- **PLIERS**
- **BARREL SWIVEL**
- **SPLIT RINGS**
- **FISHHOOK**
- **HOLE PUNCH PLIERS** (for Lure 2)

Lure 1:

1 Use the scissors to cut off the top and bottom of the can. Cut out your spinner shape from the aluminum.

2 Place the shape on scrap wood and use the hammer and nail to punch a small hole in the spinner ⅛ inch from the edge. Set the spinner aside.

3 From here, you'll be assembling the lure from the bottom up (with the hook added later), sliding all the components onto the looped wire shaft or craft wire.

4 Slide the squid, feathers, or any other dangly fish bling onto the wire.

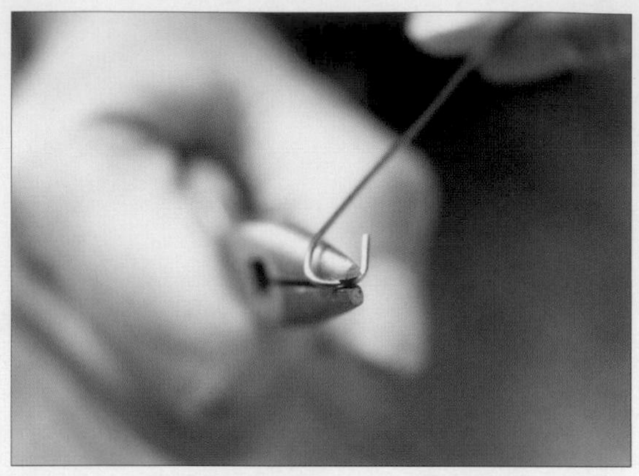

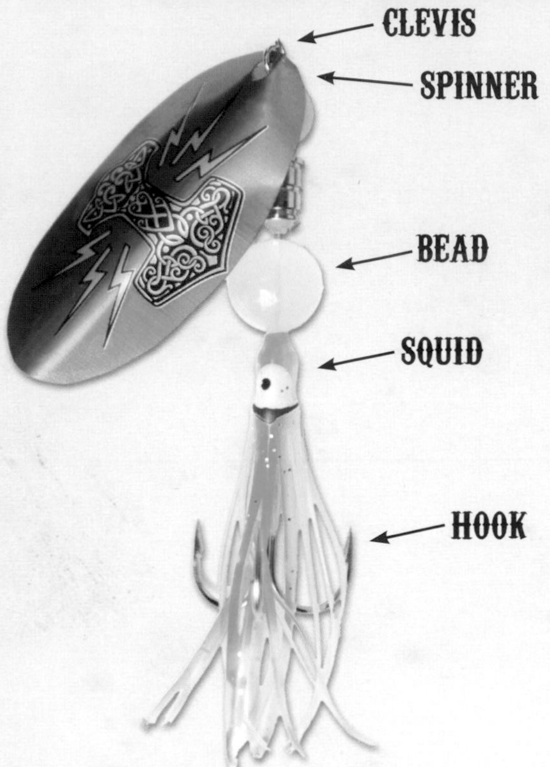

5 Add the beads.

6 Slide the spinner onto the clevis, and then slide the clevis onto the wire.

7 Using the pliers, bend your wire at the top into a loop and wrap it around the main shaft twice to secure it.

8 Clip the barrel swivel to the top of the loop.

9 Attach a split ring to the bottom loop and thread the hook onto it.

Lure 2:

1 Using the hole punch pliers, punch holes into the top and bottom edge of the bottle cap.

2 Attach split rings through each of the holes.

3 Attach a hook to one split ring and a barrel swivel to the other.

BEER CAN BIRDHOUSE

Hansel and Gretel may have had their gingerbread cottage in the woods covered in candy and sweets, but if you wanted to tempt me for fattening up it would have to be with a house made of beer cans and bottles.

While I'd love to give my little bungalow the same treatment as John Milkovisch's Beer Can House (page 120), my landlord isn't so hip on the idea. Instead I settled for making little beer can homes for the birds who visit my yard.

A couple of tips for keeping your guests happy: Make sure to punch holes for drainage in the bottom of the can. You don't want water collecting inside and mildew growing. Also, don't hang these in the sun. The aluminum will heat up pretty quickly in direct light and you and your feathered friends probably don't want fried eggs.

SUPPLIES

- 2 BEER CANS
- HAMMER AND NAIL
- SCISSORS
- PAPER HOLE PUNCH
- 1 (3-INCH-LONG) PENCIL OR DOWEL
- HOT GLUE GUN
- PHOTOCOPIER
- PENCIL
- PUSHPIN
- 18 INCHES OF THIN WIRE
- 2 BRADS
- DRIED GRASS, SMALL TWIGS, OR OTHER NATURAL MATERIAL

1 Turn one can upside down and punch five holes in the bottom, using the hammer and nail.

2 Put a small puncture hole in the side of your can, then enlarge with the scissors to make an opening for the birds to get in.

3 Using the hole punch, make a hole ½ inch beneath your door. Insert your pencil into this to serve as a perch. Secure it into place with hot glue.

4 Use the scissors to deconstruct the second can by taking off the top and bottom and cutting down the length of it to make a flat panel.

5 Copy the birdhouse roof template (page 90) and cut it out. Trace the pattern onto the can panel and cut it out. Using the pushpin, poke two small holes and insert the thin wire into each. Secure the wire to the underside of the roof with small knots and reinforce it with hot glue.

6 Bring the flat edges of the can together so that they form a cone with sides overlapping about 1 inch at the bottom. Use the hole punch to make two holes in the roof where the sides overlap, and secure with brads. Squeeze hot glue into the top of the seam and press into place.

7 Hot glue the roof onto the house can. Fill the floor of the can with nesting materials and hang in a shady spot.

hazed
& infused
dry hopped ale
Boulder, Colorado
12 FL. OZ.
Boulder Beer Company
Boulder, Colorado
12 FL. OZ.

BIRDHOUSE ROOF

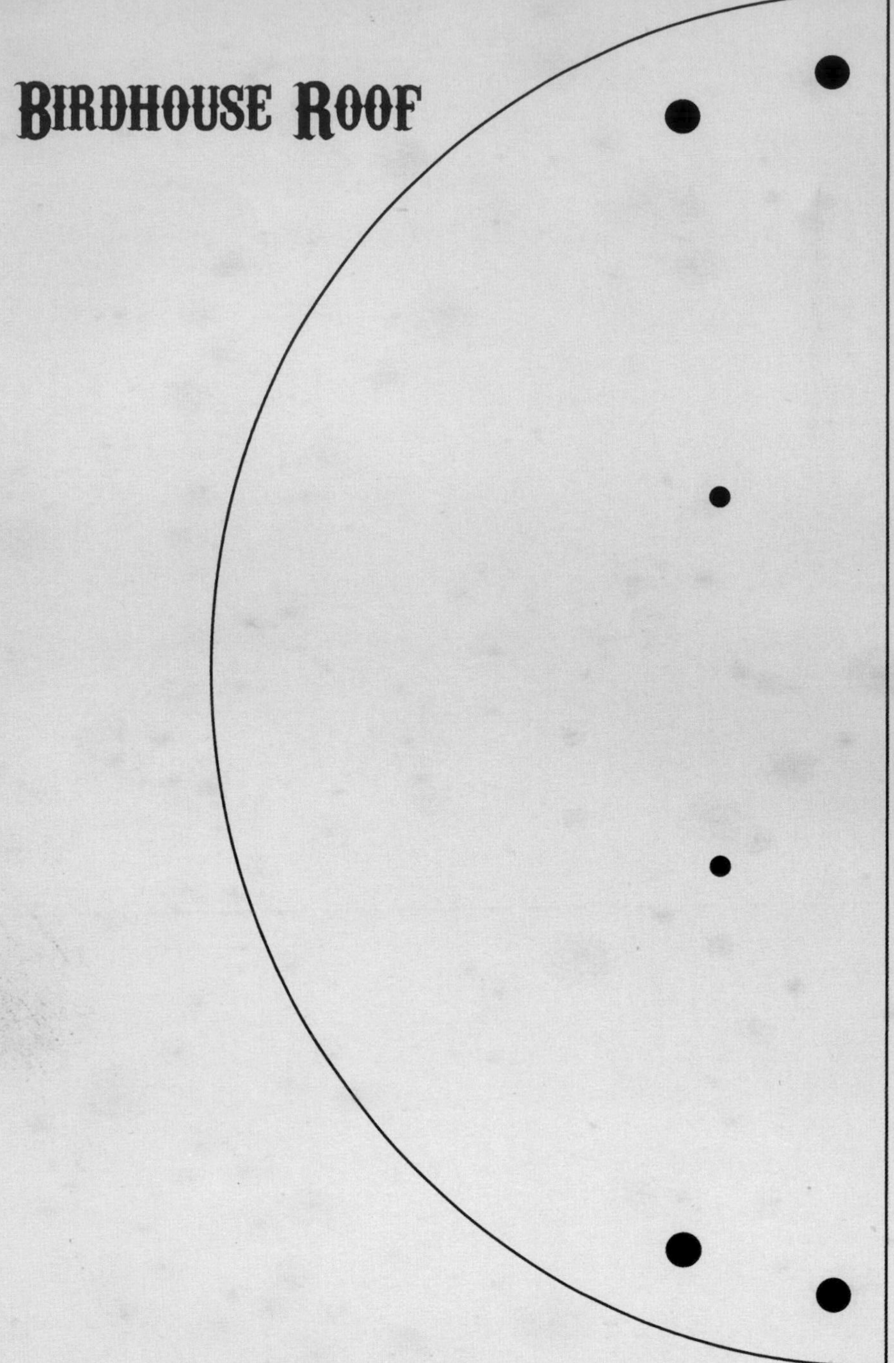

Drinking Games Travel Case

Supplies

OLD SUITCASE

DRAW HASP or suitcase latch

RULER

PENCIL

SCISSORS

FABRIC to line your case and for the partition panel, plus 1 yard of fabric for two checkers totes and lining two dice cups

STRAIGHT PINS

IRON AND IRONING BOARD

HOT GLUE GUN

13+ BEER CANS OF ONE COLOR, for the backgammon board and one dice cup

13+ BEER CANS IN A CONTRASTING COLOR, for the backgammon board and one dice cup

PHOTOCOPIER

6-INCH SQUARE OF CARDBOARD

PAPER HOLE PUNCH

BRADS (optional)

SEWING MACHINE

26 INCHES OF 1/4-INCH-WIDE GROSGRAIN RIBBON, for drawstring bags

15 BOTTLE CAPS OF ONE COLOR, for game tokens

15 BOTTLE CAPS IN A CONTRASTING COLOR, for game tokens

1/2-INCH-THICK PLYWOOD, to fit inside dimensions of suitcase

WOOD SAW

6 INCHES OF 1-INCH-WIDE GROSGRAIN RIBBON

12 INCHES OF THIN ELASTIC CORD

STAPLE GUN

BOTTLE OPENER

30 INCHES OF 1-INCH-WIDE ELASTIC

10+ CANS, for the checkerboard

One of my favorite finds in college was a retro travel bar in a plastic suitcase. In addition to a shaker and two glasses, it had space to stow your hooch and mixing tools. I love the idea of taking the party on the road and wanted to expand a bit further on the theme for this book. This large suitcase carries it all—a backgammon board, and a partition that holds checkers on one side and a bottle opener and five large cold ones on the other. Best of all, there is room for a folding vintage luggage stand I found at a thrift store and sawed down to fit.

Because it's hard to find a case with a lid and bottom the same size, I made my hinges detachable for a level backgammon board when opened completely, and the lid can get flipped over to convert to a handy table and space for the inevitable game of quarters. As old suitcases come in a variety of sizes, my directions are pretty general, giving you room to customize.

Instead of using store-bought fabric, I used empty burlap sacks from a coffee roaster down the street—cheap and stylish! If upholstery isn't your bag, you can paint the inside of the case instead of relining it.

1 Open a beer and put on your thinking cap. This ambitious project is going to take lots of measuring and planning. Take note of how the original lining fits inside the suitcase. More likely than not, you'll want to use a similar layout when putting in new fabric.

2 Remove the old hinges from the back of the case and replace them with draw clasps or suitcase latches, found at the hardware store.

3 Gently tear out the old lining, saving the pieces to use as templates for cutting and folding the new fabric. Alternately, you can paint the inside of your case if interior upholstery isn't your thing.

LINE THE CASE:

1 Measure the interior dimensions for cutting the lining and add ½ inch all the way around for fold allowances.

2 Measure and cut out the fabric. Fold down and pin the outside edges to create a ½-inch seam all the way around. When working with rounded or uneven edges, sometimes you get a little excess fabric in the folds. Trim the excess fabric and press down the seams with a hot iron.

3 Starting from the center of the case and then working your way to the side edges, use hot glue to hold the fabric in place.

MAKE THE BACKGAMMON SET:

1 Use the scissors to deconstruct your backgammon beer cans as described on page xiv. You'll need at least twelve of each brand

BREWING CO.
WOMEN ENJOYING BEER

for the board, and contrasting colors are best. Copy the template onto paper and cut it out. Check the size for fit. You'll need to fit six of the points (triangles) across the width of each suitcase side. I varied the size of my points, making one color taller than the other, but really it is a style choice on your part. I also went a step further and made slightly larger triangles, using the plain, matte inside of the beer cans as a contrast to make my triangle designs stand out. Depending on how you cut your cans, you might need to collect extra beers to make those twenty-four additional shapes.

2 Hot glue the metal points to the board.

MAKE THE DICE SHAKERS:

1 Copy the dice shaker template onto paper and cut it out.

2 Trace the template onto the cardboard and cut it out.

3 Trace the template shape onto a piece of fabric that is ¼ inch larger all around than the actual shape. Cut it out.

4 Hot glue the fabric to the cardboard. Cut slits into the selvedges, fold the fabric over to the back side of the cardboard, and hot glue it into place.

5 Repeat steps 1 through 4 to make a second shaker base.

6 Deconstruct two more beer cans, taking off their top and bottom and leaving a large rectangle to match each color of points on board. Depending on how your cans look, you may want to use four cans for this, so you'll only be using pretty labels and not looking at UPC codes and warning notes. Check the cans for fit around the cardboard bottom. You'll want at least 1 inch of space for overlap on the sides. If you need to add extra aluminum to increase the length, cut a section from the second can and overlap by about 1 inch, mark spacing, and use the hole punch to make two overlapping holes in the cans. Secure in place with brads.

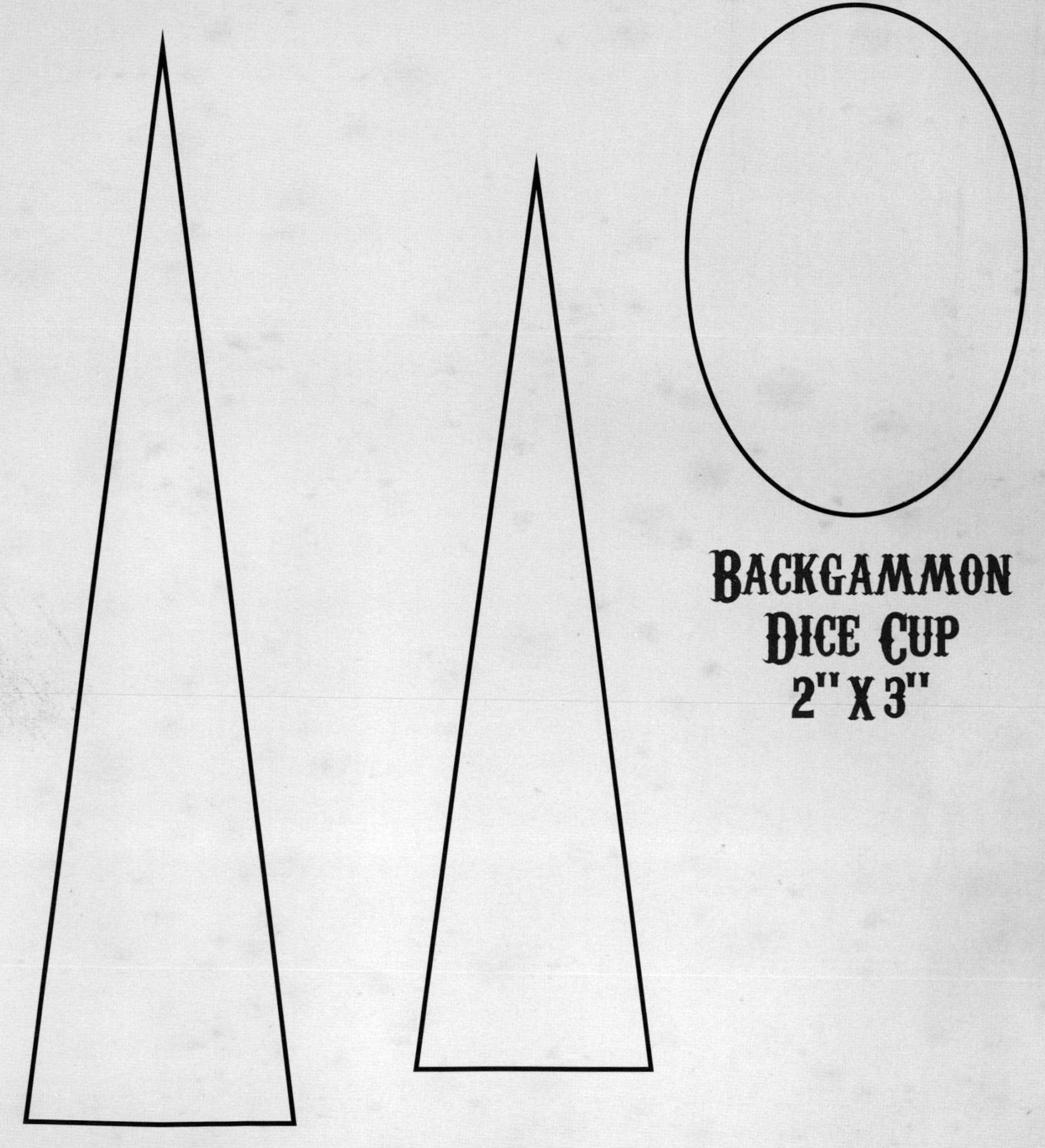

BACKGAMMON TRIANGLES

7 Cut two pieces of fabric that are 1 inch taller than the height of the cans.

8 Fold the fabric over ½ inch at the top and press the seam with a hot iron.

9 Lay the cans face up onto the fabric and fold the ½-inch seam over the top. Use hot glue to secure the fabric in place on the front side and back.

10 Wrap the cans around the sides of the cardboard pieces. Hot glue up the sides of the can at the overlap.

MAKE DRAWSTRING BAGS FOR THE GAME PIECES:

1 Decide how big you'd like your bags. Cut a piece of fabric that is double the finished height plus an additional 2 inches high, with ½ inch extra on each side for the side seams.

2 Fold down the fabric ¼ inch on each side and press the seams with a hot iron.

3 Fold the fabric in half lengthwise with the wrong sides facing and press the bottom seam.

4 Turn the fabric with the right sides facing and fold down the top seam ½ inch. Press it, fold it over another ½ inch, and press again. Stitch this seam into place at the bottom edge. Repeat for the opposite side.

5 Sew the side seams together, stopping just below the top hem. Turn the fabric right side out. Thread 13 inches of ribbon through the top hem and tie off the ends.

6 Make a second bag. Fill each with fifteen bottle caps.

MAKE THE BEER HOLDER PARTITION:

1 Cut a small sheet of plywood to fit inside your suitcase. You'll want to give it at least a ½-inch gap of extra space on all sides. Decide whether you'll line the partition with fabric. I like the finished look of the fabric, but you can certainly go with a painted wood surface instead.

2 Cut two pieces of fabric to line the partition. They should be 1 inch wider all the way around than the piece of plywood you'll be covering.

3 Lay the first piece of fabric face down on your work surface and place the partition on top. Make small notches in the corners for folds, then fold the fabric onto the board and hot glue it into place.

4 Fold the 1-inch grosgrain ribbon in half and glue the ends onto the back of the partition at the top edge with 2 inches of loop exposed. This pull tab will help you remove the partition from the case.

5 Place the second piece of fabric face down on your work surface and fold over 1 inch at both the top and bottom. Iron the seams down. Notch the fabric at the corners and fold it down 1 inch on the right and left sides. Press these seams down, too.

6 With the right side facing, determine your layout for the elastic bottle holders. My suitcase isn't huge, but it still restrains five beers, which is fine, as I'm more than happy to carry the spare from the six-pack in my free hand. You'll also want to figure out where you want to string your bottle opener. Mark this spot on the back side of your fabric.

7 Make a small incision in the bottle opener hole and thread the thin elastic cord through it. Pass the elastic through the hole in the bottle opener and back through the hole to the back of the fabric. Tie it in a knot and reinforce the knot with hot glue.

8 Run a bead of hot glue around the back edges of the partition and press the square of fabric into place.

9 Make a 1-inch slit in the fabric cover at the bottom center of the partition. Put a dab of hot glue on one end of the 1-inch-wide elastic and slide it into the slit, pressing the fabric down into place. Grab an empty

beer bottle and place it at the base of your partition. Wrap the elastic over it snuggly. Place a bead of hot glue where the elastic meets the fabric. Repeat this step with as many bottles will fit comfortably onto the partition. Cut a small slit in the top of the fabric partition where the tail end of the elastic meets it. Put a dab of hot glue on the elastic and slide it into the slit, pressing the fabric down on top. If you painted your plywood partition, follow the instructions for spacing with the bottles, using a staple gun to staple the elastic to the plywood between each bottle instead of hot gluing it.

MAKE THE CHECKERBOARD:

1 Cut sixty-four 1-inch squares of aluminum from the deconstructed beer cans. You can use two contrasting colors of cans, or the front and back sides of the same brand.

2 Lay the squares out on your partition in an eight by eight grid and attach with hot glue.

Caldera

BEER CAN STRING LIGHTS

Whether it's barbecue season or the holidays, you've probably got a set of outdoor lights that could benefit from some upcycled beer can couture. And while these strands make excellent party lights at night, they look equally cool in the daytime, when you can admire the fine design on your favorite brands. Pick a beer to match your patio decor or mix it up as I did for a cornucopia of colors. Besides the case of beer you'd be drinking anyway, the only supply you'll need is a box of brads from the office store, making this craft can glam on the cheap!

1 Copy and cut out the pattern from page 100.

2 Use the can opener and scissors to remove the top and bottom of each can and make a cut down the sides.

3 Flatten the resulting aluminum panels.

4 Trace the template onto each can panel and cut out.

5 Punch out holes A, B, and C.

6 Line up holes A and B, put a brad in through the front, and open it on the inside.

7 Adjust the shade until the overlapping scallops are aligned.

SUPPLIES

PHOTOCOPIER

SCISSORS

CAN OPENER

ENOUGH BEER CANS FOR YOUR LIGHTS
(my strand required 25)

PENCIL

PAPER HOLE PUNCH

1 STRING OF OUTDOOR GLOBE LIGHTS
(1½ inches in diameter)

50 BRADS,
or 2 brads per light

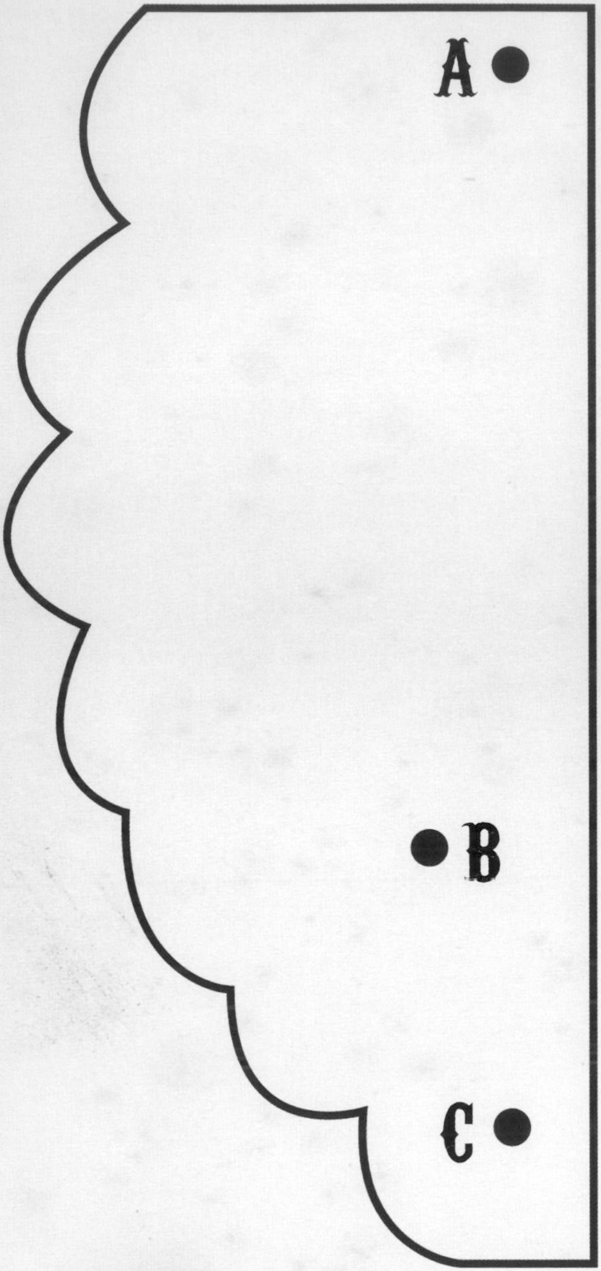

A

B

C

8 Punch a hole through hole C into the aluminum beneath it. Put a second brad through this hole.

9 Making sure your lights *are not plugged in,* unscrew a bulb from the strand and slide a shade over the base. Screw the bulb back into place.

10 Repeat with the remaining bulbs. Dig into that second case of beer when you're completely finished.

Belgians

Crisp tasting, sometimes with a **sour bite,** Belgian beers **have a** complex, **sophisticated flavor** that can come from **open tank fermentation** — *and* — **barrel aging.** The following **projects** reflect old-world **charm, and a** penchant for suave accessorizing.

WEDDING NIGHT BOTTLE CAP GARTER

This is a fetching little gift for the bride, and perhaps a sweet reminder of the first beer you shared together. Bonus points go to the crafter who uses a blue cap for the centerpiece or borrows the cap from a friend. Whether you use old caps or new, you could cover a lot of bases with some planning. And though this beer craft accessory is going to look stunning on the lady's leg, it's going to look extra sexy hanging from the rearview mirror of your chariot. Beer Crafts classy—that's how we roll.

SUPPLIES

BOTTLE CAP

HOT GLUE GUN

FAKE FLOWER (made of fabric)

PLAIN GARTER OR A 22-INCH LENGTH OF SEQUINED ELASTIC

NEEDLE AND THREAD, OR SEWING MACHINE (optional)

1 Fill the bottle cap with hot glue and let cool.

2 Glue the cap into the center of the flower and let cool.

3 Fold the garter belt in half to determine the center point.

4 Glue the flower to the garter belt at the center point.

5 If you are using sequined elastic, you'll want to stitch the garter together with right sides facing and then sew down the selvedges (the extra bits on each side of your seam). If you are lazy, like me, you'll sew the seam only, then hot glue the selvedges in place, tucking the frayed edge down underneath.

6 Open a beer to celebrate your good fortune.

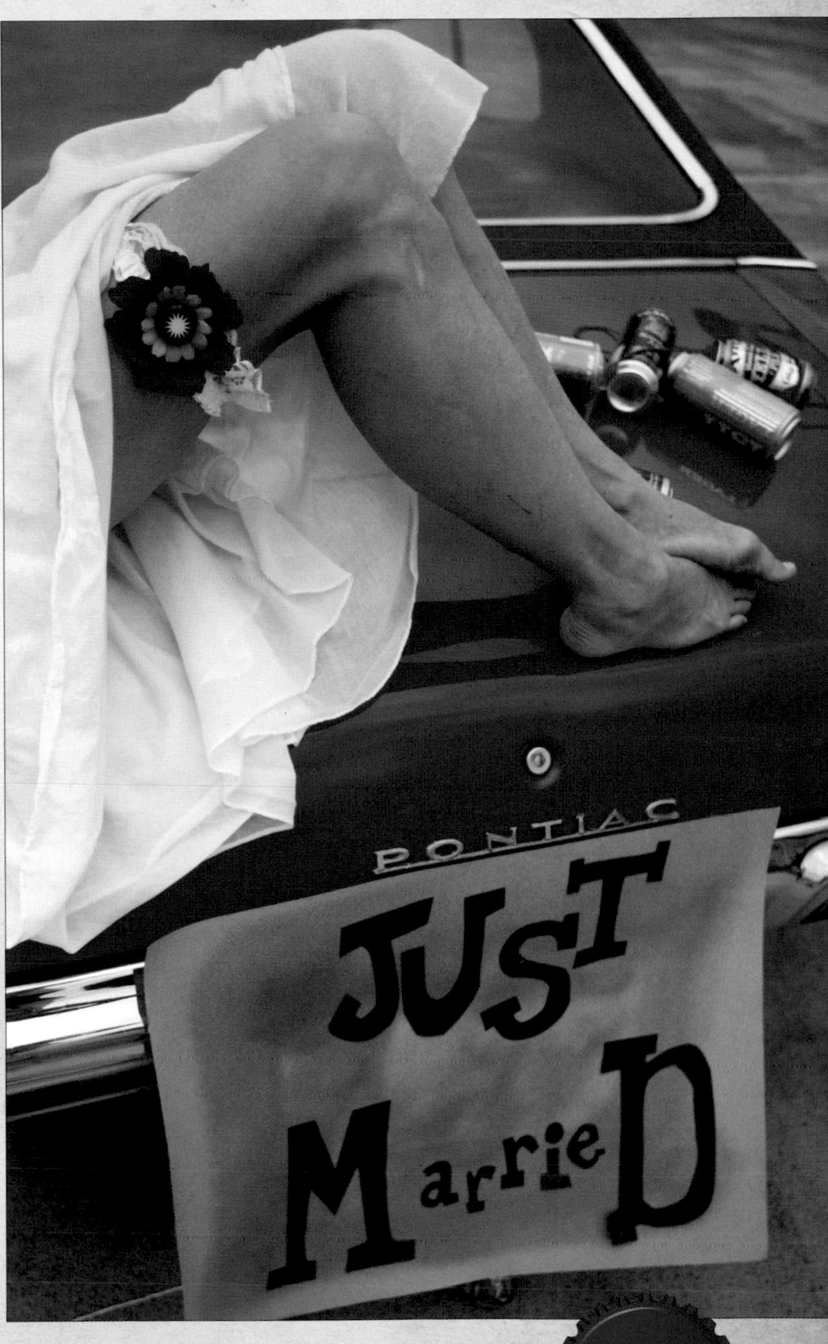

TINY CHAIR FROM A CORK CAGE

This is not the most practical craft, unless you happen to be two inches tall, but it's a great party trick and will certainly impress all the ladies in the bar. These tiny chairs look absolutely darling in a dollhouse and are the perfect excuse for sampling a host of Belgian beers, which get sealed up with corks and cages rather than metal bottle caps.

SUPPLIES

WIRE CUTTERS

METAL CORK CAGE
from a fancy bottle

PLIERS

How to

1 Using the wire cutters, snip the large wire circle at the bottom of the cage and pull it out.

2 Use the pliers to flatten this piece as much as possible. After the kinks have been straightened out, bend the wire into an arch for your chair back, or give it a loop with a twist to make a café-style chair.

3 Twist the ends of your arch to the top of the two legs of your chair.

4 Adjust the legs so the base stands straight on a flat surface.

Bottle Cap Cufflinks

Every now and again we have occasion to get dressed up, such as weddings and funerals. If your friends are anything like mine, there is usually a lot of great beer at either event. Heck, I'd even be on time for my own funeral if I knew there'd be a good beer on tap; otherwise, I'll probably take my sweet time getting there. Regardless of the occasion, if you're wearing a tux, you've got a great excuse to bust out these snappy cufflinks. They take about thirty seconds to make, and all you need is a couple of six-packs to outfit all your groomsmen with gifts, or to leave your pallbearers with a sweet memento to remind them of your excellent taste in beverages.

Supplies

HOT GLUE GUN

2 CUFFLINK BASES
(found online, or from bead stores or craft shops)

2 BOTTLE CAPS

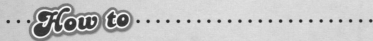

1 Have a beer and contemplate the big day, with a special toast for your friend being honored/mourned. Tell some favorite stories and drink the second beer.

2 With hot glue or other strong glue, attach the cufflink bases to the insides of the caps.

NEW BELGIUM
BREWING

Bottle Cap Button Covers

This is a great craft for fancy jackets that have superfluous buttons sewn on the sleeves, or jackets with extra-large buttonholes. As a bonus, it is about as challenging as opening a beer with a pop-top.

Some things to keep in mind: This works better with flat buttons; you may want to cut off your old buttons and replace them with flat ones—the kind with a shank protruding on the bottom, not those with holes in the face. If you're going this route, glue the cap to the new button first, then sew it into place so there is less chance of getting hot glue on your garment.

This is ideal for jacket buttons that are just for show, but you can do it with functioning buttons, too. Before gluing caps through working buttons, make sure the cap will actually fit through your buttonhole. This really only works well on jackets with extra-large holes. You could try expanding your buttonholes, but you'll probably ruin your shirt.

Also, for Pete's sake, even if you've had a few beers and it seems like a good idea, don't glue down the caps while wearing the jacket. You're begging to get burned. Ouch!

Supplies

HOT GLUE GUN

ENOUGH CAPS TO COVER YOUR BUTTONS

1 Glue an empty bottle cap onto each of your buttons and allow them to cool. It's that easy. And don't you look nice?

Bottle Label Wallet

Because I like to spend all my pocket money on fine beer, it's only fitting that my wallet artfully represent its true purpose—stashing my cold cash until it's time for the next six-pack run. My design is pretty simple, but depending on how many labels you use, you can add lots of extra pockets for credit cards and your driver's license. The size of your wallet will depend on what type of labels you use. You can use my measurements as a guide, but any size will work. I picked out two labels for five types of beer and sat down to work with a roll of clear packing tape.

Supplies

RULER

SCISSORS

CLEAR PACKING TAPE

10 BEER LABELS BROKEN DOWN AS FOLLOWS:

- **4 LABELS THAT ARE 4 X 3½ INCHES**
- **2 LABELS THAT ARE 3½ X 3½ INCHES**
- **2 LABELS THAT ARE 3 X 3½ INCHES**
- **2 LABELS THAT ARE 2½ X 3½ INCHES**

CRAFT KNIFE (optional)

How to

1 Open a beer.

2 Measure and cut an 8½-inch length of clear packing tape and lay it on your work surface, sticky side up. Measure and cut another 8½-inch strip and lay it beneath the first, slightly overlapping. Repeat this until you've got a sheet of tape "fabric" that is about 4½ inches tall.

3 Place two of your largest labels face down on the tape fabric with a ¼-inch gap between them. Place two more labels of the same size face up on top of the first pair of labels.

4 Make a second sheet of tape "fabric" the exact same size as the first, and place it sticky side down on top of the first, sandwiching the labels inside. Trim away the excess tape "fabric," leaving a slight tape border around the edges. You've now made the outside and base of your wallet.

5 Make another tape "fabric" 8½ inches long, and this time about 4 inches tall. Lay it on your work surface sticky side up.

6 Place two 3½ x 3½-inch labels face up onto the tape "fabric," leaving a ¼-inch gap between them. Make another sheet of tape "fabric" of the same size and lay it sticky side down on top, covering the front of the labels. Trim away the excess tape.

7 Set this second part of the wallet on top of the base with the labels facing up, making sure the ¼-inch center gaps are aligned. With the bottom edges aligned, tape the front and back of the pocket at the right and left edges.

8 Make tape "fabrics" for the remaining two sets of labels and attach those pockets to the wallet base as in step 7. When all four layers are attached at the sides, tape the bases to the inside pockets at the bottom edge.

9 Measure and cut a thin strip of packing tape 4 x ½ inch. Place this tape on the center gap of the inside of the wallet just underneath the top pocket opening. Wrap the excess around to the front of the wallet or trim it at the bottom edge.

10 Check the pockets for fit. If some are too big to fit credit cards, carefully trim away the excess tape with the craft knife.

11 Fold the wallet in half, and you're ready to roll. The best part is that you can easily mend your accessory with extra tape when it starts to wear out.

PIRAAT
ALE
PRODUCT OF BELGIUM
330 ml / 11.2 fl. oz.
PIRAAT
ALE
LAGUNITAS
NEW BELGIUM
elevated for a while. So, what's on the tube..?

CONEY ISLAND
CRAFT LAGERS
CRAFT LAGERS

BOTTLE CAP PENDANT AND EARRINGS

For all its simplicity, the bottle cap pendant makes an elegant and bold statement, declaring your devotion to a beloved brewery. I've included a couple of different methods for making necklaces: an easy one that uses hot glue, and another that involves punching a hole in the cap. Either technique will work well, and it is really a matter of personal preference and what tools you have on hand.

A single bottle cap makes an elegant statement, and multiple caps look great on anklets or on wire hooks for earrings. For a fancy night of pub crawling, I like to gussy up a bit and wear my necklace of a dozen caps and colors, with extra beads and charms to dress the piece up. It looks smokin' hot with a white T-shirt.

SUPPLIES

BOTTLE CAPS

HOT GLUE GUN (for the hot glue technique)

PULL TABS FROM CANS OF BEER (for the hot glue technique)

HOLE PUNCH PLIERS (for the punch technique)

PLIERS (optional)

JUMP RINGS

NECKLACE CHAIN of desired length

BALL AND COIL EARRING HOOKS

ASSORTED BEADS AND BLING (optional)

HOT GLUE TECHNIQUE (PENDANT ONLY)

Before I got a nice tool to poke holes in caps, this was my technique for making pendants. I am a huge fan of the glue gun, and anything that lies around my house for a couple days is fair game for getting glued to something else. (Anything without a pulse, that is.) I also like the idea of using the pull tab as part of the jewelry hardware. My recycling is doing double duty, and it's one less thing in the landfill.

1 Prep your bottle cap with hot glue. Once the cap has cooled and the glue is solid, lay a pull tab face up on top of the glue. You want it face up so that the smooth side of the tab lies against your skin when the necklace is completed.

2 Position the tab so that the top of the metal extends slightly past the top edge of the bottle cap, creating a gap where you'll attach the jump ring.

3 Add a second thin layer of glue to secure the pull tab in place.

4 Using pliers or your fingers, open the jump ring and thread it through the top of the pull tab. Close the ring.

5 Thread your chain through the jump ring.

PUNCH TECHNIQUE (PENDANT OR EARRINGS)

For this, you are simply putting a small hole in the cap near one of the edges. You'll want your hole to be large enough to thread a jump ring into, and fairly close to the edge so the ring can move easily. Hole punch pliers are a special tool, but boy, are these great for getting the job done. They make a perfect hole every time, exactly where I want it, and it takes seconds. When I decided to write this book I bought a fancy punch that scrapbookers like to use, called a Crop-A-Dile, which has two heavy-duty punches on it in two sizes, and it also sets grommets and snaps. This ended up being a great investment, as I used it for a number of projects in the book.

1 Use the hole punch pliers to punch a hole in the bottle cap close to the edge.

2 Continue as for steps 4 and 5 of the hot glue technique, threading the jump ring through the hole you punched in the cap.

EARRINGS

1 Punch holes in two caps. Thread a ball and coil earring hook through each jump ring. You can punch a second hole at the bottoms of your caps and attach beads, chains, and other bling.

You can expand on the necklace by using the punch technique to punch holes in the sides and bottoms of several caps and attaching beads, chains, and other bling, as shown.

Stouts and Porters

ROBUST AND WARMING, THESE FULL-BODIED DRINKS PACK IN DEEP BASE — *and* — CARAMEL NOTES. LIKE THE BEERS THAT INSPIRED THEM, THE FOLLOWING PROJECTS ARE COZY REMINDERS OF HEARTH — *and* — HOME.

NINKASI BREWING
EUGENE OREGON
RADIANT ALE

UINTA
HOP NOTCH

Big Amber
RED MENACE

Scotch
Style Ale
PIKE
KILT
LIFTER

Beer Box Tiara

Sometimes a girl likes to feel pretty. Whether at a special celebration, or just when she's playing Queen for a Day at home, these paper crowns are sure to draw the attention of loyal admirers and worthy subjects. The stunning tiaras won't have you breaking the royal bank, either, as the main supplies are a plastic headband, a six-pack carrier that you've probably got in the recycle bin right now, and, of course, glitter—lots and lots of glitter.

1 Open a beer. You'll want to relax and ponder your design options a bit.

2 Use the scissors to cut out your desired shapes from the box. I look for one central piece about 8 inches wide, for the base of my tiara.

3 Set the headband on a work surface and hot glue the central cardboard piece to it.

4 Hot glue the accent shapes behind the central piece. Tall and thin ribbon shapes, radiating stripes, or clusters of circles look great for this.

5 Place your tiara on a paper towel. Brush on some craft glue wherever you want extra sparkle, then sprinkle liberally with the glitter. Allow to dry, then dust off the excess onto the paper towel. You could also use glitter glue for highlights. Allow to dry.

6 Use craft glue to attach sequins or other small treasures. Allow to dry.

Supplies

- SCISSORS
- 1 EMPTY SIX-PACK CADDY
- 1 THIN PLASTIC HEADBAND
- HOT GLUE GUN
- PAPER TOWEL
- CRAFT GLUE
- PAINTBRUSH
- GLITTER, SEQUINS, GLITTER GLUE, AND OTHER EMBELLISHMENTS

John Milkovisch's Beer Can House

Being a beer crafter doesn't involve special skills or talents. It's an everyman (or woman) occupation, packed with pleasure, and the resources are readily available. As with so many other hobbies, there are some folks who take tinkering with cans and bottles to artistic extremes.

John Milkovisch was just that sort of guy. With an equal supply of ingenuity and time, and an ever increasing collection of empty beer cans, John converted his Houston bungalow on Malone Street into a folk art masterpiece with the outside of his house and property tastefully decorated with what Ripley's Believe It or Not! estimates is fifty thousand beer cans.

Working nights and on weekends, John covered the exterior walls with cut and flattened cans, then moved on to decorating planter boxes, making garden art, dangling curtains of can tops from the roof eaves, and stringing garlands of aluminum from the trees.

His wife, Mary, put her foot down at the front door, declaring the inside of the house her turf, and in the interest of a harmonious marriage, John kept his ambitious beer crafted embellishments strictly on the outside. Looking back at his visionary achievement, Mary speculated his motivation came from "not wanting to mow the grass."

John's workdays were spent doing interior upholstery work for the Southern Pacific Railroad, and he was especially skilled in linoleum tile cutting and design. Examples of his stunning floor work are in several rooms of his home.

John had an excellent sense of humor and unassuming perception of his magnum opus. When asked about all the folks who'd come to see his home, he played it cool, saying, "I had no idea that people would be so interested in beer cans. I wouldn't travel around the block to see something like that." He spent more than eighteen years building his dream, before moving into a retirement home after a stroke. Claiming his preferred brand of beer was "whatever was on sale," John played no favorites.

If there was a Beer Crafter Hall of Fame (and there should be), John would top the list. Ambitious and dedicated, he built his dream one beer at a time, illustrating for the rest of us just how far our collection can go.

These days, John's Beer Can House is curated and maintained by the Orange Show Center for Visionary Arts, which promotes other awesome Houston creations, including the Orange Show, which is an outdoor folk art environment built by Jeff McKissack to honor his favorite fruit, and the annual Art Car Parade, where more than 250 embellished, blinged, and funked-out vehicles cruise through the city to an appreciative crowd of more than thirty thousand during a full weekend of curiosities and events.

DESCHUTES BREWERY
SIERRA NEVADA
NEW BELGIUM
WIDMER BROTHERS BREWING
BRIDGEPORT
Full Sail
WIDMER BROTHERS

John Milkovisch-Inspired Bottle Cap Curtain

Truly a craft for the beer enthusiast, this stunning curtain transforms your voluminous cap collection into a magnificent conversation piece. You can drape it across a window or in front of a shower curtain, hang it against a wall for a dramatic statement, or suspend it from runners for a completely unique room divider. Best of all, since the only additional supplies you'll be needing are paper clips and hole punch pliers, your objet d'art is only going to set you back a couple of bucks in pocket change, freeing up the rest of your hard-earned dough for a couple of quality six-packs that are completely display worthy.

Because making something this impressive can be time consuming, you'll probably want to have a few friends over to help you out—just like an old-fashioned sewing bee, but with beer.

Supplies

- A ZILLION BOTTLE CAPS
- HOLE PUNCH PLIERS
- 500 OR MORE PAPER CLIPS

How to

1. Open a beer and one for your friends, too. This is going to take a team effort.

2. Punch four holes into the edge of your bottle cap: one at the top, one at the bottom, and one on each side.

3. Thread a paper clip completely through each hole.

4 Punch four more holes in another cap and connect it to one of the paper clips from your first cap, with the tops of the caps all facing the same way. Similarly connect three more caps to the remaining paper clips.

5 Keep punching holes in the caps and connecting the clips and caps until your curtain is the size you want it to be.

BOTTLE LABEL COASTERS AND TASTING NOTES

As you may suspect, I have an extensive collection of labels from favorite beers. Part of me hangs on to them for decoration's sake alone, but I also keep them around for reference. There's nothing like a little solid evidence to kick start the brain into a trip down memory lane.

Turning your labels into coasters with tasting notes on the back is a great way to track your favorite brews. I usually make two coasters for each beer I sample, writing down my own notes on one and leaving the other blank. When I'm having tasting parties with friends, I bust out the blanks, where they can take their own notes using dry-erase markers, which wipe clean for the next soiree.

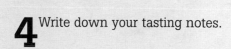

SUPPLIES

- **LARGE POT**
- **1 OR MANY BOTTLES OF BEER**
- **SCRAP PAPER**
- **BLANK WRITING PAPER**
- **PEN OR FELT-TIP MARKER**
- **SCISSORS**
- **PHOTOCOPIER** (optional)
- **LAMINATING MATERIALS** (optional)
- **PINKING SHEARS OR OTHER FANCY PAPER CUTTERS**

1. Fill the large pot with water and soak the bottles for several hours or up to overnight.
2. Gently peel off the labels and lay them on the scrap paper to dry.
3. Trace the labels onto the blank writing paper and cut out along the outlines.
4. Write down your tasting notes.
5. Alternatively, you can copy the tasting template from this book and enlarge or shrink it to fit on the back of your labels.

DUBHE
Imperial Black IPA
RAYON VERT
BELGIAN-STYLE PALE ALE
UPRIGHT
BELGIAN
Red brow
STYLE
APPEARANCE
SMELL
TASTE
RATING

6 Laminate the labels (most copy shops can do this if you lack the materials). Cut out the laminated labels, leaving a ¾-inch margin.

7 Use pinking shears or fancy paper cutters to create a decorative border.

BOTTLE GIFT BAGS AND COZIES

For the best flavor, you've got to serve your beer at its proper temperature. More and more often, beer companies will list recommended serving temperatures—and even what type of glass to use—on the label. I like my pilsners and IPAs almost icy, my stouts just a tad cooler than room temperature, and my Belgians somewhere in between.

Getting your beer temperature right and keeping it there can be a bit tricky, especially an on hot day. That's why I'm a big fan of cozies, which keep your beer cool and look pretty fabulous, too. My favorite cozies are made from the hacked-off sleeves of old sweaters. I use kid-size sweaters for normal-size beer bottles, and grown-up sweaters for the 22-ounce variety. A simple stitch sewn at the bottom edge of a sleeve and a little ribbon transform your thrift store find into a fetching gift bag, which I seal closed with a pull-tab cinch.

SUPPLIES

✻ FOR THE BEER COZY ✻

RULER

SCISSORS

CHILD-SIZE SWEATER (something with ribbed sleeves works great)

SEWING MACHINE (optional)

✻ FOR THE GIFT BAG ✻

RULER

SCISSORS

SWEATER WITH SLEEVES no larger than 12 inches around at the widest point

SEWING MACHINE

18 INCHES OF ½-INCH-WIDE RIBBON

PULL TAB from a beer can

BEER COZY

1 Open a beer.

2 Measure and cut off one sleeve of the sweater about 4½ inches from the wrist opening.

3 For a hemmed edge, take the cut end of the fabric and roll it under ½ inch to the inside of the sleeve, then stitch around the edge. Of course, hems are an option, and a frayed edge on your cozy can look pretty cool, too.

4 Put the cozy over your beer and enjoy.

Gift Bag

1 Normally I'd start with, "Open a beer," but because this is a gift for a friend, we'll just skip ahead to step 2.

2 Measure and cut off one sleeve of the sweater about 10½ inches from the wrist opening.

3 Using the pattern on page 133 for reference, cut an arch shape into the wider opening of the sleeve.

4 Turn the sleeve inside out and sew a line about ½ inch from the cut edge.

5 Turn the sleeve right side out. About 2 inches down from the top of the sleeve, cut ½-inch slits every inch around the sleeve.

6 Thread the ribbon through the slits, leaving two equal tails at the starting and ending point. Thread the ends through the pull tab, insert a beer, and cinch closed.

GIFT BAG
(ENLARGE 127%)
10"
STITCH HERE
CUT HERE

MINE
OURS

BOTTLE CHARMS

I have a hard time keeping track of my beer at parties. I'll get to gabbing with friends, set down my cold one on the table, and then have no idea which bottle among the throng belongs to me. Back in the day, I'd pretty much drink whichever beer was closest, figuring the fuller, the better. That was up until I discovered that some people will use bottles for emergency ashtrays—lesson learned, the hard way. I've tried the old trick of peeling the label off my beer, but even that can lead to some confusion about which beer belongs to whom. With this project, we'll all know which beer is his, hers, and theirs, the rest being all mine.

1 Open a beer. Think about ownership. This is *your* beer; it belongs to you. Think about how you'll mark your territory.

2 Copy the cap templates with a laser photocopier or design your own, to create six cap inserts.

3 Cover the front and back sides of the copied or designed cap inserts with clear packing tape. Cut out the cap insert shapes and use the glue stick to tack them to the inside of the caps.

4 Fill the caps with sealant and let them dry overnight or as recommended by the manufacturer's directions.

5 Turn over each cap and attach a chain attachment with hot glue. Let cool.

SUPPLIES

6 BOTTLE CAPS

LASER PHOTOCOPIER AND PAPER

CLEAR PACKING TAPE

SCISSORS

GLUE STICK

RESIN EPOXY SEALER OR GLOSSY ACCENTS, a clear, dimensional embellishment sealer

6 JEWELRY-BACK CHAIN ATTACHMENTS

6 JUMP RINGS

ELASTIC THREAD (see Note)

ASSORTED BEADS AND CHARMS

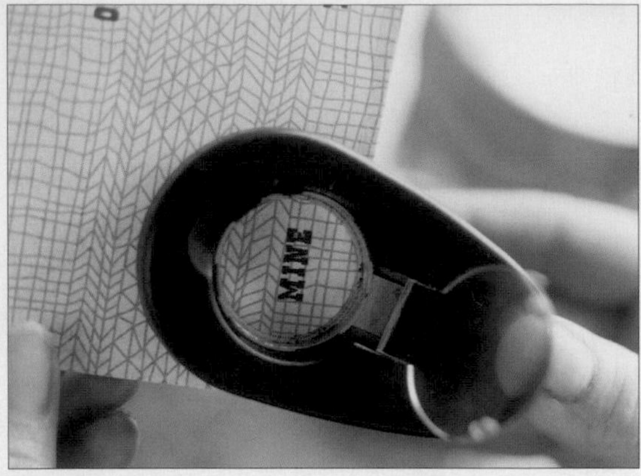

6 Attach a jump ring to the back of each cap.

7 Tie a knot in a piece of elastic thread and string on enough beads to fit halfway around a beer bottle snugly. String on a cap and additional beads and tie off. Repeat for the remaining five caps.

It's really important to use elastic thread for the charms. The tension from the elastic keeps the charm held up against the bottle neck instead of sliding forward and smacking you in the face when you go to take a swig—yet another lesson I learned the hard way.

YOURS

HIS

HERS

OURS

MINE

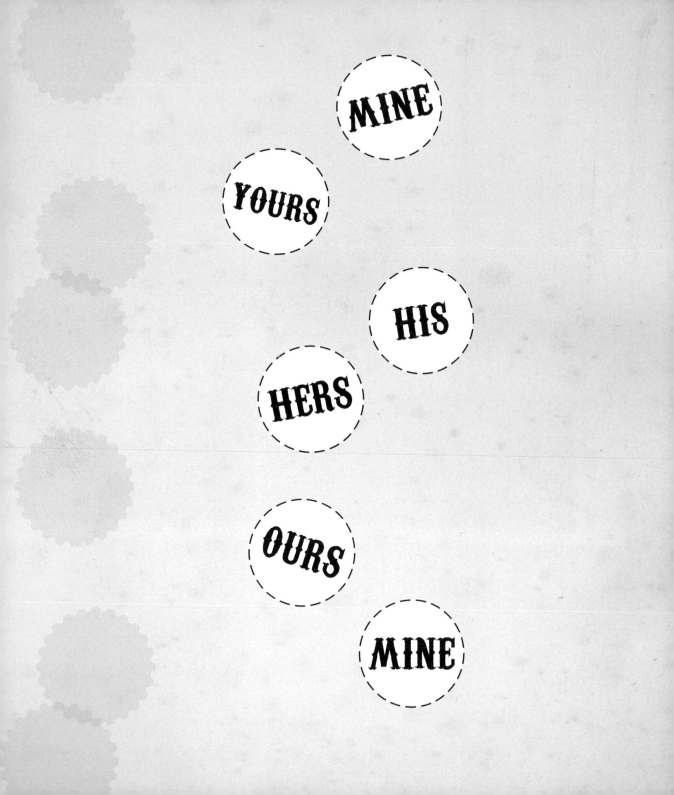

I ♥
BEER

I ♥ Beer Pendant

You love your beer; yes, you do. This affair of the heart is no secret. Your bartender knows it. The guy at the liquor store knows it. How about shouting it out loud and proud to the rest of the world? You can put all sorts of fun messages in a cap, as well as photos and artwork. Most craft stores carry paper punches that will cut paper perfectly to fit inside your cap, and you can go to town with your artsy self and throw in a little glitter and rhinestones, while you're at it.

Make sure you're printing your work with a laser printer. Some resins and sealers will make the ink from ink-jet printers run, and you'll end up with a blurry pendant. If you're unsure about your ink running, you can either test by making an extra copy and immersing the image in resin OR cover your print, front and back sides, in packing tape to make sure you don't get a bleed.

SUPPLIES

LASER PHOTOCOPIER

RESIN EPOXY SEALER OR GLOSSY ACCENTS, a clear, dimensional embellishment sealer

BOTTLE CAP from a favorite beer

HOT GLUE GUN

PULL TAB from a can of beer, **OR 1 PENDANT BACK**

PLIERS (optional)

JUMP RING

NECKLACE CHAIN of desired length

1 Copy the template from the book with a laser photocopier. Cut out the design. Put a small dot of resin on the inside of your bottle cap and place the design on top. Allow to dry.

2 Fill the cap with sealant and let it dry overnight or as recommended by the manufacturer's instructions.

3 Hot glue the pull tab or pendant back to the back side of your cap.

4 Using pliers or your fingers, open the jump ring and thread it through the top of the pull tab. Close the ring.

5 Thread your chain through the jump ring.

I ♥ BEER

BEER ME

SOURCES

Craft Supplies

COLLAGE

1639 NE Alberta St.

Portland, OR 97211

503-249-2190

www.collagepdx.com

Fishing Supplies

JAX OUTDOOR GEAR

1200 N. College Ave.

Fort Collins, CO 80524

1-800-987-9059

970-221-0544

StoreManager01@jaxmercantile.com

www.jaxmercantile.com

Hardware

McGUCKIN HARDWARE

2525 Arapahoe Ave., Unit D1

Boulder, CO 80302

1-866-248-2546

303-443-1822

www.mcguckin.com

Metric Conversions

To Convert	**Multiply**
Inches to centimeters	Inches by 2.54

APPROXIMATE METRIC LENGTH EQUIVALENTS

Length	
1/8 inch	3 millimeters
1/4 inch	6 millimeters
1/2 inch	1.25 centimeters
1 inch	2.5 centimeters
2 inches	5 centimeters
2 1/2 inches	6 centimeters
4 inches	10 centimeters
5 inches	13 centimeters
6 inches	15.25 centimeters
12 inches (1 foot)	30 centimeters

ABOUT THE AUTHOR

Former professional chef and current crafter extraordinaire, Shawn Gascoyne-Bowman dallied in a promising East Coast film career, but decided to chuck it away to raise a demanding and ungrateful family and an ill tempered dog. Attached to her glue gun in a meaningful yet painful way, she spends her days skulking in Portland, Oregon, writing, making stuff, and drinking awesome beer. Follow Shawn at **www.beer-crafts.com**.

ABOUT THE PHOTOGRAPHERS

Laura Sams and Robert Sams are the sister/brother team behind the camera. When they're not photographing beer crafts for adults, they are the creative masterminds and designated drivers behind Sisbro Studios, a business dedicated to creating films, books, music, and educational presentations to help children of all ages learn about nature (and laugh along the way). Check them out at **www.sisbro.com**.